Stepping through the Psalms and the Proverbs

MW00467376

ALAN ENGLE

ISBN 978-1-0980-5292-8 (paperback)
ISBN 978-1-0980-5293-5 (digital)

Christian Faith Publishing, Inc.
832 Park Avenue
Meadville, PA 16335
www.christianfaithpublishing.com

All scripture verses are taken from the New King James Version (NKJV). Copyright 1982 by Thomas Nelson Inc. Permission has been under gratis use guidelines. All rights reserved.

Printed in the United States of America

To my deceased wife, Lisa
March 27, 1956 to July 30, 2018

Introduction

● ●

Like many retired pastors, I embarked on a writing project. It was prophesied to me that this is what I would do next. Before I started, God showed me a title for the book, *Stepping through the Psalms and the Proverbs*. I had developed a love for certain passages in both books. Even if no one else ever read *Stepping through the Psalms and the Proverbs*, I have enjoyed a journey through these books, extracting those verses that particularly had my attention. My request from God is that the Holy Spirit would guide me and give me the right words to write. I had no desire to add to or detract from the Word of God.

My objective was to extract the most powerful words of the writers to me and expound upon them. There are words of inspiration interwoven in the Psalms and the Proverbs for people like you and me. I wanted to express those thoughts in today's vernacular in light of hope, encouragement, and joy.

This commentary is not a scholarly work but an inspired one. I have simply let the words come off the page and followed the leading of the Holy Spirit. Jesus had not arrived on the scene when the Psalms and the Proverbs were inspired, but today we read the verses through the lens of Jesus the Messiah present with us. I encourage everyone to read the Psalms and the Proverbs for themselves and to appreciate and be enlightened by them.

I invite you the reader to sit with the Holy Spirit and study the books together. I hope you will enjoy your steps through the Psalms and the Proverbs as much as I have and continue to do so.

Alan Engle
January 9, 2020

Step 1

• •

But his delight is in the law of the Lord,
and in His law he meditates day and night.
He shall be like a tree
planted by the rivers of water,
that brings forth its fruit in its season,
whose leaf also shall not wither;
and whatever he does shall prosper.
—Psalm 1:2–3 (NKJV)

This verse suggests that we can take delight and pleasure in the Word (law) of the Lord. It is agreeable to our soul to open the Word and to enjoy spending time reading it. The Word is living and powerful to change our thinking, our emotions, and our choices. It is the very breath of God and contains His DNA.

To walk in God's blessings, study the Word, and listen to the counsel of the Holy Spirit, we will be like a healthy plant that is in good soil, watered, taking in sunlight, budding and bringing forth fruit in season. However, we will not wither and die before our time.

The good soil is the Word of God. That Word is watered by the Holy Spirit and prospers in the light of the Son of God. In His presence is to be near to Him and constantly refreshed.

We are not swayed because our roots are deep into the Word of God. The Word rules our thinking and behavior. The world's counsel is considered but does not catch us up. Sin and judgment have no place in our life. Your focus and compass comes from the Word of God.

Step 2

• •

But You, O Lord, are a shield for me,
my glory and the One who lifts up my head.
I cried to the Lord with my voice,
and He heard me from His holy hill. Selah
I lay down and slept; I awoke, for the Lord sustained me.
I will not be afraid of ten thousands of people
who have set themselves against me all around.
—Psalms 3:3–6 (NKJV)

Isn't it good to know that when we call upon the Lord in our distress, He hears us? God is never too busy or too far away to answer our call for help. And the Holy Spirit is our shield, comforter, and safety in the time of trouble, persecution, or temptation. He will never leave us or forsake us.

We are to ask God, and He will answer. We can tap into a hope that is supernatural, but those who do not know Him choose not to access. He knows our every thought, but He wants us to put those requests into words so that we hear them and so does God.

Most of us spend eight hours of our day in rest and sleep. The devil will try to visit you in the nighttime hour when you are most vulnerable. But the Lord watches out for us and is a guard for us in our sleep. Now when we awake, we realize that He has sustained us throughout the night.

Christians are in a spiritual battle whether they know it or not. There is an army of evil aligned against us, and we know the devil is out to steal, kill, and destroy us. We need not fear because our God is greater than the devil, and when we speak the name of Jesus, he must flee.

Step 3

● ●

> But let all those rejoice who put their trust in You;
> let them ever shout for joy, because You defend them;
> let those also who love Your name
> be joyful in You.
> For You, O Lord, will bless the righteous;
> with favor You will surround him as with a shield.
> —Psalm 5:11–12 (NKJV)

Distrust, doubt, and unbelief are the greatest hindrances to God working in our lives; they squash the joy and blessings from the Lord. We are the righteousness of God and are to live like we know it. Jesus paid the price of our sin, and when we accepted Him as our Lord and Savior, we were made righteous.

We love the name of Jesus and the Person of the Godhead who is the Son of God. Jesus showed us a trust in the Father and a love for Him that we are to model. We are to love Jesus just like He loved the Father; loving God in that manner makes it easier to love others as well.

Joy doesn't have to be manufactured; it comes as a result of trust and love. A personal relationship with our Lord Jesus stirs up the love necessary to walk in God's love and safety. Favor with God comes from trusting in Him completely to protect us in any circumstance.

Because we are in the kingdom of God, we have righteousness, peace, and joy. The Holy Spirit reminds us of our righteousness and releases a peace in our soul so that joy abounds. Peace, joy, and safety are found in the shadow of God's wings.

Step 4

● ●

> O Lord, our Lord, how excellent is Your name in all the earth,
> who have set Your glory above the heavens… When I consider
> Your heavens, the work of Your fingers, the moon and the stars,
> which You have ordained, what is man that You are
> mindful of him, and the son of man that You visit him?
> For You have made him a little lower than the angels,
> And You have crowned him with glory and honor.
> You have made him to have dominion over the
> works of Your hands; You have put all things
> under his feet.
> Psalm 8:1, 3–6 (NKJV)

When we look to the sky on a clear night, what beauty and immensity is experienced! This unique earth is so small in our galaxy and yet teeming with life like no other planet. The beauty of a colorful sunset reflects the artistry of the Creator God.

That same God who fills the universe has come to live in our hearts. How awesome is that? We are an important part of His kingdom, and we are significant to Him even though our lives are so small and fleeting in the grand scheme of things.

When we gave our lives to Jesus Christ, we became an active part of the great plan and design of God. He knew us before we were born. It might seem difficult to understand why an almighty Creator God would consider our lives important, but He does! It's because of His great love for mankind that He thinks about us.

We have been made a little lower than the angels but given the ability to understand the deep things of God. We have been given power to heal the sick, to help the lost, be saved, and to destroy the works of the enemy. When we do the works of God, we share in His glory and honor.

Step 5

• •

I will praise You, O Lord, with my whole heart; I will tell of all Your marvelous works. I will be glad and rejoice in You; I will sing praise to Your name, O Most High… The Lord also will be a refuge for the oppressed, a refuge in times of trouble. And those who know Your name will put their trust in You; for You, Lord, have not forsaken those who seek You.
—Psalm 9:1–2, 9–10 (NKJV)

There is power in praise and worship, whether it is done individually or corporately. Praise that comes from deep within us is pleasing to the Lord. It has the power to cleanse and purify our souls. When we overflow with praise to the Lord, others hear it and are influenced by it.

Praise to the Lord is a choice we make that comes from a heart that is set apart for the Lord. God is not listening for a beautiful voice but is looking to the heart. Praise is a remedy for the oppressed and persecuted saint. It releases joy supernaturally and fills the empty and troubled heart.

God knows when we are in the grip of oppression and persecution. These are times when it's hard to find a voice of praise. But He is saying to us to trust Him, and He will get us through. God wants us to turn to Him in the midst of temptation and sin.

What a friend we have in Jesus! He knows our temptation and trouble because He experienced it all. He also knows that we cannot resist in our own power for very long. We must turn to a higher power that has defeated the devil and provided a safe refuge for us.

Step 6

• •

But I have trusted in Your mercy; my heart shall
rejoice in Your salvation. I will sing to the Lord,
because He has dealt bountifully with me.
—Psalm 13:5–6 (NKJV)

The fool has said in his heart, "There is no God."
—Psalm 14:1 (NKJV)

In mercy, we have been spared of the punishment we deserved because of our rebellion toward God and sin against Him. Through the mercy of God, He sent His Son, Jesus Christ, to earth to atone for the sins of mankind. To all who receive His blood bought sacrifice, we can take joy in our salvation.

In grace of God, we have received the rewards of salvation we did not deserve. Jesus took the punishment for our sins, and we received the blessings of salvation. Heaven rejoices in every soul that is saved and living for God. A life that was destined for hell has been turned around to eternity in heaven.

The believer looks to heaven and says, "Thank you, Jesus, for saving me." The unbeliever in rebellion, ignorance, and selfishness says, "There is no God." Believers know there is a God because the Holy Spirit has drawn them to Jesus Christ, and Jesus has come to live inside of them.

We know about lost souls because our souls were once lost. We pray for the lost that their eyes might be open to the truth of Jesus Christ, Son of God, and that they might look at the creation and know that God is the Creator. We pray that the lost might come to know that God is alive, real, and desiring so much that they will also come into His kingdom.

Step 7

• •

Lord, who may abide in Your tabernacle?
Who may dwell in Your holy hill? He who walks
uprightly, and works righteousness, and speaks
the truth in his heart.
—Psalm 15:1–2 (NKJV)

The kingdom of God is open to all who have accepted Jesus as Lord and Savior and King. It is when Jesus is King and has come to live inside of us that the kingdom is in us and all around us.

Must we do the works of righteousness to be admitted to the kingdom? The price of admission is by believing in your heart and speaking with your mouth that Jesus is Lord is the price of admission. You became righteous when you accepted Jesus Christ into your life.

We live freely in the kingdom, and we live and move and have our being in the kingdom because of Christ in us. Our lives, thoughts, words, and actions are according to scripture and the leading of the Holy Spirit.

Does this seem too simplistic and unrealistic? Not really because any other efforts on our parts besides believing takes us into works of righteousness on our efforts. Salvation and righteousness are free gifts for those who believe in the sacrifice of Jesus and accept it. Only Jesus can set us free; nothing or anyone else cannot accomplish it. We can't take credit for what Jesus has done for mankind, only accept it. Once accepted, then the journey of true life begins.

Step 8

● ●

O Lord, You are the portion of my inheritance and my cup;
You maintain my lot.
The lines have fallen to me in pleasant places;
yes, I have a good inheritance.
I will bless the Lord who has given me counsel;
my heart also instructs me in the night seasons.
I have set the Lord always before me;
because He is at my right hand I shall not be moved.
—Psalm 16:5–8 (NKJV)

We are part of the family of God. We are adopted as sons and daughters. We are brothers and sisters to Jesus because He is the Son. We have the same Father now through a spiritual rebirth. That includes a wonderful inheritance.

In the family of God, Jesus is our teacher, counselor, and leader. He goes before us, and we follow Him. The voice of the devil is ignored and not followed. We don't listen to the lies of the devil when truth has been made available.

It's easy to be swayed and influenced by a so-called truth that is relative. It can change from day to day, by who is pronouncing it colored by their personality and opinions. But the truth that comes from God and is printed in His Word is trustworthy and never changing.

We are not to be moved off of God's truth. It is rock-solid, informative, and a compass for providing direction. It is as deep as we choose to go and challenges us to go deeper. The student of the Word is enlightened by it and stirred to learn more.

Christian martyrs have risked their lives to smuggle the Word of God into forbidden places. A memorized passage is enough to sustain a persecuted Christian. A few pages of the Bible are enough to sustain an underground Bible study.

Step 9

Therefore my heart is glad, and my glory rejoices; my flesh also will rest in hope. For You will not leave my soul in Sheol, nor will You allow Your Holy One to see corruption. You will show me the path of life; in Your presence is fullness of joy; at Your right hand are pleasures forevermore.
—Psalm 16:9–11 (NKJV)

The heart of the believer rejoices and is glad because Jesus is not in the grave. The Father raised Him up after three days in the tomb, and Jesus is alive forevermore. We died with Christ and were buried with Him and were raised to eternal life in heaven.

But we must not forget that wide is the road of destruction, and many travel on it. That road leads to a cliff of destruction with no turning back. Along the way there is sorrow, sin, regret, and frustration.

The only wise solution is to find the narrow path of life and get on it. Those who seek the Lord find the narrow path and allow the Holy Spirit to direct their way.

Along that path the presence of the Lord is experienced. Joy, love, and peace fill the heart of the believer in His presence. There is no confidence and hope like this available on the wide road.

We have to stay on the narrow path. Veering slightly off the path are barriers and obstacles that slow the journey. So to get back on the path of life, the presence of God brings relief and success. Only Jesus show us that path and keeps us on it.

Step 10

● ●

Uphold my steps in Your paths,
that my footsteps may not slip.
Keep me as the apple of Your eye;
hide me under the shadow of Your wings,
as for me, I will see Your face in righteousness;
I shall be satisfied when I awake in Your likeness.
—Psalm 17:5, 8, 15 (NKJV)

Thank you, Lord. You keep us on the straight and narrow path. It's only by the power of the Holy Spirit and the love and leadership of Jesus that our footsteps do not slip. It is the enemy's plan to get us off course by using all kinds of devious tricks. We are in a battle that the devil has already lost!

To be the apple of God's eye is favor and amazement. The Creator God sees us a precious and valuable. He has a plan for us that is beyond our imagination. He keeps encouraging us and picking us up when we stumble. He is our great protector.

At the end of this earthly life, we will see Jesus face-to-face. We will recognize Him, not from earthly sketches but a spiritual sense of His presence. We have walked several miles with our Savior in this life. The future in heaven is a reason to stand up and shout, "Hallelujah!"

What a joy to see all our friends and family in heaven. There will be no regrets like we experience in this earthly life. Get ready to hear, "Well done, good and faithful servant."

Step 11

• •

I will love You, O Lord, my strength. The Lord is my rock
and my fortress and my deliverer; MY God, my strength, in
whom I will trust; MY shield and the horn of my salvation,
my stronghold. I will call upon the Lord, who is worthy
to be praised; SO shall I be saved from my enemies.
—Psalm 18:1–3 (NKJV)

We love the Lord because He means so much to us. On our own, we
are weak, but walking in the Spirit releases His strength in us. Jesus is
the rock, and on that solid foundation, we will build our lives. Our
God is a strong tower to which we run, and He is our deliverer from
any addiction, habit, or snare the enemy might bring.

God is our strength in any area where we are or have lack, He
supplements those things that are missing. In Christ, we can do all
things. He is our source of whatever we need and our protector. He
protects us from any attack of the enemy that would try to steal our
joy and hope. We will take joy in our salvation that has brought us
into new life and health.

No point in holding on to the things of the world or regretting
our past life because they are passing away and are temporary. God's
kingdom is growing and solid; it is an eternal dwelling place.

So in our current situation, we will call upon the name of the
Lord to keep us in the light. When things are going well, we will
praise and thank Him. He is our peace and joy, no matter what is
going on in the world.

Step 12

•••••••••••••••••••••••••••••••••

For You will light my lamp; the Lord my God will enlighten
my darkness. For by You I can run against a troop, by my God
I can leap over a wall. As for God, His way is perfect; the word
of the Lord is proven; He is a shield to all who trust in Him.
—Psalm 18:28–30 (NKJV)

Thank you, Lord, for You have turned on a lamp inside each of us.
We desire to be a light of encouragement and hope to friends and
family. If our light flickers, then we ask that You renew it from above.
People are looking to us to be strong and an example to them of the
love of God. When the darkness of sin, hopelessness, and persecution
sneak up on us, turn up our lamp.

Because of the Lord's presence in us, we have the power to overcome every obstacle in our way. What imprisoned us before is coming down, and we are no longer held back by the petty issues of life.

The way of the Lord is perfect. As we follow Him, we become
perfected and are becoming more like Him.

Jesus is the Word, and in the Word, we find the wisdom to fulfill God's plan for our life. Many who have gone before us followed
that instruction and were successful. No matter who or what comes
against us, His Word is truth, His way is light, His love never ends,
and His plan is perfect. The doors of heaven are open to us, and He
will guide us safely home.

Step 13

• •

The law of the Lord is perfect, converting the soul;
the testimony of the Lord is sure, making wise the simple;
the statutes of the Lord are right, rejoicing the heart;
the commandment of the Lord is pure, enlightening the eyes;
let the words of my mouth and the meditation of my heart
be acceptable in Your sight,
O Lord, my strength and my Redeemer.
—Psalm 19:7–8, 14 (NKJV)

When the heart is filled with the Word of God, it rejoices. The Word perfects us because it is the source of perfection. We are enlightened by reading and taking it in as food for the soul. A wise person grows wiser and stronger by spending time in the Word. A believer's heart filled with the instruction of God thinks and speaks perfectly.

Help us, Lord, to guard our tongues. May our speech come from a new and pure heart that You have given us. Let us not have loose lips and careless words; they are to be far from us and never spoken. The desire of our hearts is to edify, encourage, and build up those around us with our words. Our words are to be tools for good and not for destruction. Lord, remove from us a critical, sarcastic, and mean spirit. Purify our hearts, Lord, because that is the source of our thoughts and words.

The Lord resides in us so we have the mind of Christ. We can think and reason like Jesus and speak what He would like us to say. There is an abundance of right thoughts and correct words residing in us. Help us, Lord, to make that connection and tap into what is good inside of us. Inspire us to think and speak like heaven.

Step 14

• •

May He grant you according to your heart's desire, and fulfill all
your purpose. We will rejoice in your salvation, and in the name
of our God we will set up our banners! May the Lord fulfill all
your petitions. Now I know that the Lord saves His anointed;
He will answer him from His holy heaven with the saving
strength of His right hand. Some trust in chariots, and some in
horses; but we will remember the name of the Lord our God.
—Psalm 20:4–7 (NKJV)

God has promised to give us our heart's desires if we stay connected
to Him. One of our desires is to fulfill the plan He has for us—our
very reason for living. Let's trust Him to reveal that plan to us so we
can be working on the next part of it. God is not done with us as
long as we are alive and able. He will use us in some way to fulfill our
purpose in the kingdom. We are not created to simply breathe and
take up space.

Let's begin by praising Him for our salvation. Raise a banner
to the Lord because He has forgiven our past life and making us
righteous.

God is looking for a humble person who will say, "Here I am,
use me." Ask God to show you an eternal purpose for your life. The
things of the world are temporary and passing away. He us wants to
bring heaven to earth by using our gifts and talents to honor Him.

Can you imagine what our world would look like if each born-
again believer would do his small part in the kingdom? The puzzle is
not complete until each piece is in its proper place.

Step 15

● ●

The king shall have joy in Your strength, O Lord; and in Your
salvation how greatly shall he rejoice! You have given him his
heart's desire, and have not withheld the request of his lips. Selah
for You meet him with the blessings of goodness; You set a crown
of pure gold upon his head. He asked life from You, and You gave
it to him—length of days forever and ever. His glory is great in
Your salvation; honor and majesty You have placed upon him.
For You have made him most blessed forever; You have made him
exceedingly glad with Your presence. For the king trusts in the Lord,
and through the mercy of the Most High he shall not be moved.
—Psalm 21:1–7

We are all kings and priests in the kingdom of God. These are not
positions that we earn but because Jesus Christ is in us. Being a king
creates strength in us and as a priest releases joy. Salvation cannot be
earned; it is a gift from God through the work and death of Christ
on the cross.

We have new lives in Christ. The old lives are gone, and the new
ones have begun. As new people with new hearts, what is your desire
for this new life? The Lord will answer your question in accordance
with His will.

Blessings of goodness come from the God of goodness who is
in us. We have positions of honor in the kingdom and crowns of
gold. The challenge is not walking in pride but to do all things with
a humble spirit.

Our lives are not our own; they belong to God. This is real life,
stimulating and alert, loving, peaceful, and full of joy. God's strength
will sustain us all the days of our lives.

Step 16

• •

The Lord is my shepherd; I shall not want. He makes
me to lie down in green pastures; He leads me beside
the still waters. He restores my soul; He leads me in
the paths of righteousness for His name's sake.
—Psalm 23:1–3 (NKJV)

The Lord is in charge of our lives. We have free will, but we let God influence our decisions and choices. We are humble souls given over to the Lord in trust and obedience.

God provides for the needs of His children. He clothes them from nakedness, satisfies their hunger, and shelters them from the storm.

Not only does God satisfy our needs but provides for our wants as well. He does it out of love for His children, protects them and shows them the way to live their lives.

We were born into a world of sin and depravity. God desires to return us to a state of purity and wholeness. He knew we could not stay out of trouble on our own, so He sent His Son, Jesus, to be our substitute and example. Jesus gave His life for us so that we might have life. In Christ, we are nourished, safe, and at peace.

Once we are transformed by His grace, we are invited back into the driver's seat. But this time, we have the Holy Spirit to be our guide and to show us the way to go. Through the rest of our life, we are to give honor and glory to God. Thank you, Lord, for being our shepherd.

Step 17

Yea, though I walk through the valley of the shadow
of death, I will fear no evil; for You are with me;
Your rod and Your staff, they comfort me.
—Psalm 23:4 (NKJV)

There are places in our lives which are dangerous and threaten our very existence. One is the mission field for Christ, where persecution is intense. Another is the highway where a careless or drunk driver can end your life. Personal health can ruin your life from a diagnosis of cancer. These are just a few, but God has an answer for all of them.

First, God says, "Fear no evil," and Jesus often said, "Fear not." Fear is that emotion that often jumps up first in a bad situation. The Lord wants us to let go of fear and trust Him through it all. There is a good kind of fear that protects us in an attack from the enemy. But there is a negative kind of fear that weakens us as we trust only in our own strength. The Lord wants us to leave that fear behind and trust Him through the most difficult and life-threatening times.

God wants to move us into a place of calm, peace, and reassurance. We can develop an attitude that will get us through the bad times. And He will comfort us in any loss. Whenever you are in a place like that, God is saying, "Do not be afraid, I am with you."

Step 18

• •

You prepare a table before me in the presence of my enemies;
You anoint my head with oil; my cup runs over. Surely
goodness and mercy shall follow me all the days of my
life; and I will dwell in the house of the Lord forever.
—Psalm 23:5–6 (NKJV)

In the presence of God we are able to defend against every attack of the enemy. God has equipped us for battle, we are His armor-bearers. We are more than enough against the enemy. No matter what the enemy throws at us, he cannot stop the blessings from God coming our way.

If we stray from the path God has laid out for us, then the Holy Spirit will lead us back on course. God's forgiveness is always available to the believer who repents from sin. What a good God we serve.

This journey we are on leads us to the wide open gates of heaven. Our time on earth is short, fleeting and temporary. The Holy Spirit is assisting us to use each moment wisely. We can't change the past, because it's past, we only have the present moment and then it's past. The future is sure and established in the house of the Lord forever.

Step 19

· ·

Who may ascend into the hill of the Lord? Or who may
stand in His holy place? He who has clean hands and a pure
heart, who has not lifted up his soul to an idol, nor sworn
deceitfully. He shall receive blessing from the Lord, and
righteousness from the God of his salvation. This is Jacob, the
generation of those who seek Him, who seek Your face.
—Psalm 24:3–6 (NKJV)

When Jesus died on a cross, the veil to the inner most part of the
temple was torn open. When Jesus ascended into heaven, He entered
the throne room and sat down at the right hand of the Father. Jesus
made a way for all of us to enter into the throne room of God and
into His presence.

So who may enter and stand in that holy place? The answer is
those who have given their hearts to the Lord, who follow after Him
and live according to the Holy Scriptures. In that place, we receive
blessings forevermore.

The enemy tries to get us off course from following the Lord.
He places distractions in our way that are contrary to God. An idol is
something that distracts us and consumes us to the point of pulling
us away from the Lord.

We are a generation that lives and moves and have our being
in the presence of God. We have given our selfish rights and decisions to the leading of God. In His presence are the answers to our
questions and the solutions to our problems. Let us live in submitted
obedience to Him.

Step 20

• •

To You, O Lord, I lift up my soul.
Show me Your ways, O Lord;
teach me Your paths.
Lead me in Your truth and teach me,
for You are the God of my salvation;
on You I wait all the day.
—Psalm 25:1, 4–5 (NKJV)

The soul and the flesh are accustomed to and friendly with the old you. They controlled our life previously, and our minds were influenced by worldly thinking. The flesh and the emotions were driven by selfish motivations. Our choices and decision-making and actions were the result of these influences.

Then at the just the right moment, we were born again. We were given a new heart, and our spirit came alive. It was out with the old you and in with the new. The control center of our lives was taken over by the spirit inside of us and controlled by the Holy Spirit.

Jesus Christ came to live inside of us. A whole new way of thinking, feeling, and decision-making has taken place inside of us. Now we can say, "Show me your ways, Jesus, and teach us in the way we should go." Let godly truth and wisdom fill our hearts. Holy Spirit, help us to truly be students of the Word of God.

So it's time to say goodbye to the old and hello to the new. We are saved, redeemed, forgiven, and transformed into the people God intended us to be. But we will not be in a hurry. We will wait upon the Lord, and He will deliver us from the old ways.

Step 21

● ●

The Lord is my light and my salvation; whom shall I fear? The
Lord is the strength of my life; of whom shall I be afraid?
—Psalm 27:1 (NKJV)

Thank you, Lord, that You are the light of our lives and our salvation.
The light of the Lord has come to dwell inside of us so that we can
shine that light on others.

It is by the grace of God that we are saved today and for eternity.
No efforts on own could earn salvation and righteousness. They are
gifts of God to us who believe and receive.

Because we are filled with the light of God and saved, we have
an inner strength to face what the devil or the world might throw at
us. We can do all things through Christ who strengthens us.

We are people of confidence and boldness because we know our
God and know who we are in His kingdom. Fear has no place in us
to weaken our resolve to move forward.

Outsiders and unbelievers view us as a little strange and weird.
We see this world as temporary and know we are here for only a short
time. We view this world as a testing ground and preparation for our
destiny in heaven.

Step 22

* *

Hear, O Lord, when I cry with my voice! Have mercy also
upon me, and answer me. When You said, "Seek My face,"
my heart said to You, "Your face, Lord, I will seek."
—Psalm 27:7–8 (NKJV)

Our enemies are anyone and anything that would try to take us out
of God's will. It could be an addiction to drugs, alcohol, pornogra-
phy, etc., that has the power to possess us instead of being possessed
by our Lord Jesus Christ. We are also in a war with the powers of
darkness that are trying to lure us away from the kingdom of God.

An enemy of our soul must be defeated by the presence of God
and the power of the Holy Spirit. God's love and mercy are available
to us through the lowest and darkest of times. That is when it is time
to seek the face of the Lord when the world seems to be falling apart
all around us.

The Lord Jesus hears us when we call out to Him in distress. He
knows what we are going through because when He was a man and
He was tempted in all ways but did not sin. The Lord Almighty is
never too busy to hear our cry.

God is ever present and all-knowing and full of compassion.
He is concerned about our lives. We are in the family of God with a
loving Father who reaches out to us in our time of need.

In our own strength, we stumble and stray here on earth. But
there is coming a time in heaven when we will be relieved of all
temptation and sin and be able to sing with all the angels in praising
our God.

Step 23

● ●

Teach me Your way, O Lord, and lead me in a smooth path,
because of my enemies. I would have lost heart, unless I had
believed that I would see the goodness of the Lord In the
land of the living. Wait on the Lord; be of good courage, and
He shall strengthen your heart; wait, I say, on the Lord!
—Psalm 27:11, 13–14 (NKJV)

In our own strength, the way through life is rough and difficult, but
in the will and guidance of the Lord, it is smooth. A smooth path
is paved with faith, knowing that God is keeping us out of the ruts
and helping us over the barriers. God doesn't remove all the barriers
on a smooth path but teaches us how to manage the difficulties that
we face.

We do not lose heart with the trials of this life because the goodness, kindness, and love of the Lord surround us. We have to stay
focused on this fact and not let the circumstances take control.

In the midst of the trouble, we wait upon the Lord, count
on His strength, abide in His love, and depend on His presence.
Relief from difficulty or pain doesn't always happen instantly; it does
involve waiting, knowing that God has not forgotten us or forsaken
us in our plight.

We thank Him for standing with us, teaching us patience, giving us courage, and strengthening our hearts. The goodness of the
Lord is all around us if we just open our eyes.

Step 24

● ●

I will extol You, O Lord, for You have lifted me up, And have not let my foes rejoice over me. O Lord my God, I cried out to You, and You healed me. O Lord, You brought my soul up from the grave; You have kept me alive, that I should not go down to the pit. His favor is for life; weeping may endure for a night, but joy comes in the morning. Now in my prosperity I said, "I shall never be moved." Lord, by Your favor You have made my mountain stand strong.
—Psalm 30:1–3, 5b–7a

The Lord has rescued us from whatever the enemy has thrown our way. Remember the ways in which He has healed your body. We have been given salvation and made righteous. He has sustained us and kept us from falling away, and His favor is for a lifetime.

The favor of the Lord is forever. He does not withhold it unless we refuse to receive it. And then He is not refusing to give it, just storing it till we want it. Trials and testing are ongoing, and as we trust Him, He gets us through. No matter how hard the testing may seem, there is power and strength that brings joy and victory.

Once through a crisis, it's time to learn from it and make any necessary changes. This prepares us for the next test that will come our way. Each test provides an opportunity for us to grow and to stand strong in the Lord. As we mature in the Lord, we become steadfast in our faith and less apt to be moved off our firm foundation.

Step 25

● ●

Hear, O Lord, and have mercy on me; Lord, be my helper!"
You have turned for me my mourning into dancing; You
have put off my sackcloth and clothed me with gladness,
to the end that my glory may sing praise to You and not be
silent. O Lord my God, I will give thanks to You forever.
—Psalm 30:10–12 (NKJV)

Losses come in many ways, some by poor choices on our part and others through adverse circumstances. Wrong choices can involve drugs and alcohol, an unbridled tongue and bad spending habits to name a few. We usually cannot change the wrong choices we have made, but the Lord will help us recover and lead us to make better decisions in the future. So we say, "Lord, have mercy upon us, be a supernatural helper, and guide to us."

We live in a fallen world. Bad things will happen to good people. A cancer diagnosis can surprise us. A loss of a loved one can cause us grief. Natural disasters (fire, flood, or storms) can seriously affect our lives. We will depend on You, no matter what comes our way.

In You, Lord, we see a brighter day. We may get knocked down, but we will not stay there. With the Lord's help, we will rise up and overcome. We will let the bad things that have happened to us in the past, stay in the past, and we will live in the present.

Lord, help us to see the big picture. Let us not dwell on the small stuff but look with new lens on the current situation. May we have heaven's perspective and see our lives in a new way. Discouragement, hopelessness, and negativity have to go. They will not control us nor influence our future.

Step 26

● ●

For You are my rock and my fortress;
therefore, for Your name's sake,
lead me and guide me.
But as for me, I trust in You, O Lord;
I say, "You are my God."
My times are in Your hand;
be of good courage,
and He shall strengthen your heart,
all you who hope in the Lord.
—Psalm 31:3, 14–15a, 24 (NKJV)

In the name of Jesus, we will seek wisdom for the journey ahead. When the storms of life threaten to engulf us, we will be sheltered in the arms of the Lord Jesus. He is the rock that we stand on and the foundation of what we believe. He is our leader, and the Holy Spirit is our guide.

Others may trust in material things and governments, but we will trust in the Lord. When asked, we will declare that "Jesus is Lord over our lives."

We will not falter in difficult times because our faith is in the Lord. He gives us boldness when other people are weak. Our hearts are purified and strengthened by Him. Where else can we turn? The solutions of the world are temporary and cannot match up to the strength and power of our God.

When the situation seemed hopeless and filled with doubt, we turned to the Lord. In Him is supernatural strength and hope to get us through the darkest night.

Step 27

• •

Blessed is he whose transgression is forgiven, whose sin is
covered. Blessed is the man to whom the Lord does not
impute iniquity, and in whose spirit there is no deceit.
—Psalm 32:1–2 (NKJV)

As born-again Christians, we do sometimes go astray, say the wrong
thing, think and do the wrong things. We are tempted to sin and
sometimes give in to that temptation. God has provided a remedy for
our transgression. He has forgiven our past sins when we were saved
and has provided an ongoing solution for us in the present.

Jesus Christ took all our sins past, present, and future to the
cross at Calvary. Through His death and shed blood, we were washed
clean of all iniquity. The Father God does not count our sins against
us because Jesus has taken them all upon Himself and wiped them
out.

We turn away from all sinful behavior and walk in the righteousness that Jesus has provided. Our job is to keep walking away
from sin and not give in to it. In our own strength, we are weak and
vulnerable, but in the power of the Holy Spirit, we are overcomers.

When we do sin, we are to confess it to the Father, receive forgiveness, and walk in the Spirit. God knows we struggle in this life
and do not always live a clean life. So He has put in place a system of
forgiveness and is faithful and just to forgive us of all iniquity.

With a new heart and a pure spirit, we control our thoughts,
guard our tongues, and keep our actions acceptable to God. Every
day we live more and more like Jesus until we meet Him one day
face-to-face in heaven where there is no sin. Hallelujah!

Step 28

● ●

I will instruct you and teach you in the way you should go; I
will guide you with My eye. Do not be like the horse or like the
mule, which have no understanding, which must be harnessed
with bit and bridle, else they will not come near you. Many
sorrows shall be to the wicked; but he who trusts in the Lord,
mercy shall surround him. Be glad in the Lord and rejoice,
you righteous; and shout for joy, all you upright in heart!
—Psalm 32:8–11 (NKJV)

We are to be students of the Word of God, constantly studying our
Bibles for instruction in the way we are to go. Scripture is the very
breath of God, and it is one of the ways God teaches us if we will
humble ourselves before Him. Let us put aside our preconceived
notions and be a blank slate before Him.

The Word of God has the power to permeate our wrong thinking and change it. It can break down the barriers to truth. The Holy
Spirit guided the writers of the Bible to record what God would say
to us. So let's allow the same Holy Spirit to write on the tablets of
our hearts.

Don't let stubbornness or pride get in the way of understanding.
The Bible is rich in wisdom and instruction for us today. Just when
we think we know it all, that is the time to open the Word and be
enlightened.

We are to understand what God is saying to us today. Let's trust
Him because He knows what is best for us. Be glad that He has rescued you from the powers of darkness and take joy that you are the
righteousness of God.

Step 29

● ●

Rejoice in the Lord, O you righteous!
For praise from the upright is beautiful.
For the word of the Lord is right,
and all His work is done in truth.
He loves righteousness and justice;
the earth is full of the goodness of the Lord.
—Psalm 33:1, 4–5 (NKJV)

Let us join the chorus of believers who sing and play instruments of praise. To sing unto the Lord releases an expression of love and appreciation for Jesus Christ. Praise and worship music hurts the ears of the enemy and drives him far from us. Let words of praise come from our mouth during personal and private meditation.

The Word of God reminds us to sing unto the Lord out of our righteousness. As we experience the joy of the Lord, words of praise come from our lips. It is in the Lord that we move, live, and have our being.

Our lives are not our own. We were chosen by God to be a blessing to others. May the same love that God has shown to us be expressed by our lives. We are the righteousness of God. We live by His truth and His peace surrounds us. The world can only observe and criticize these things, but we can experience and immerse ourselves in them. There is pain and hardship in this life, but through it, all the believer is lifted up by the love, peace, and joy that comes from God, and we can call it good!

Step 30

● ●

He fashions their hearts individually;
he considers all their works.
Behold, the eye of the Lord is on those who fear Him,
on those who hope in His mercy,
to deliver their soul from death,
and to keep them alive in famine.
Our soul waits for the Lord;
He is our help and our shield.
For our heart shall rejoice in Him,
because we have trusted in His holy name.
Let Your mercy, O Lord, be upon us,
just as we hope in You.
—Psalm 33:15, 18–22 (NKJV)

God knows us inside and out, the good and the bad; nothing is hidden from Him. He is all knowing of every thought and intention of our hearts. God sent His Son, Jesus, to take every dark and evil part from us. Jesus gave us new life so that we are not burdened by the mistakes and stains of the past.

Now we can be the clay formed and molded by the Master Potter. We can be the masterpiece that He always intended us to be. We are new creations in the hands of the Creator. So we can stop striving in our own strength and live out our days in the guidance of the Holy Spirit in accordance with God's plan.

God is pleased with those who have finally yielded and are obedient to Him. We are those who reverence the almighty God. We put our hope in Him and receive His mercy. We are delivered from the plan of the enemy and are prospering in the presence of the Lord.

What joy we experience by trusting and hoping in the Lord! He has sent the Holy Spirit to be our guide. We can relax in His arms because we are no longer adrift in a sea of hopelessness and fear.

Step 31

I will bless the Lord at all times; His praise shall continually be in my mouth. My soul shall make its boast in the Lord; the humble shall hear of it and be glad. Oh, magnify the Lord with me, and let us exalt His name together. This poor man cried out, and the Lord heard him, and saved him out of all his troubles. The angel of the Lord encamps all around those who fear Him, and delivers them.
—Psalm 34:1–3, 6–7 (NKJV)

Our minds think of the goodness of God, and we thank Him for His many blessings to us. Our hearts exalt the Lord, and our mouths speak praises to Him when cued to do so. We magnify the name of Jesus privately and corporately. What a great place to be when we are aligned with God! The praises come easily! God does not withhold any good thing from us, so let's not stifle our worship and thanksgiving to Him. This is the atmosphere that the believer can walk in.

When the enemy surrounds us, we call out to Jesus for His strength. When we are tempted to the breaking point, we draw on the power of the Holy Spirit to resist. We call out to God, and He hears us and delivers us from all of our trouble.

We have personal angels who have been assigned to us. They are to assist us when the attack of the enemy intensifies. The angel of the Lord fights for us and protects us. We are in a battle that Jesus has already won. We belong to Him and share in His victory.

Step 32

• •

Who is the man who desires life,
and loves many days, that he may see good?
Keep your tongue from evil,
and your lips from speaking deceit.
Depart from evil and do good;
seek peace and pursue it.
The eyes of the Lord are on the righteous,
and His ears are open to their cry.
Many are the afflictions of the righteous,
but the Lord delivers him out of them all.
—Psalm 34:12–15, 19 (NKJV)

We desire to live a good life, to fulfill and live out our days the best we can. With God's help, that is possible. The devil is out to steal, kill, and destroy us, so we have to stay out of His grip.

We are to watch carefully what we say. Our conversation can bring curses on us by speaking negatively. Words spoken carelessly about ourselves or others can be condemning and damaging. There is also power in the tongue to speak with encouragement and hope.

There are times when it seems attacks from the enemy are on every side. He knows what we are going through and is there to help. We are not shy to call upon Him and to admit we don't have all the answers.

God may not remove all of our afflictions, but he provides a way to get through them. Let's face it. Tests and trials cause us to grow to where we can handle whatever life sends our way!

Step 33

• •

Your mercy, O Lord, is in the heavens; Your faithfulness reaches
to the clouds. Your righteousness is like the great mountains;
Your judgments are a great deep; O Lord, You preserve man and
beast. How precious is Your lovingkindness, O God! Therefore
the children of men put their trust under the shadow of Your
wings. They are abundantly satisfied with the fullness of Your
house, and You give them drink from the river of Your pleasures.
For with You is the fountain of life; in Your light we see light.
—Psalm 36:5–9 (NKJV)

In the Lord is the source of true life. The abundance and extent of
this amazing life is immeasurable. There is satisfaction and peace in
knowing we can have true life in Christ.

Jesus Christ took the punishment we deserved so that we could
enjoy life and life eternal we did not deserve. His faithfulness can be
depended on no matter what is going on around us. The righteousness of God was given to us because we accepted Jesus Christ as Lord
and Savior. God's judgments are sure yesterday and forever. His love
for us has no boundaries and is freely given.

His pleasures are available to us right where we are. We can
jump into the river of life in this place and right now. The source of
His goodness to us is unlimited and continually flowing. We have
come out of darkness into His marvelous light. It is a light that cannot go out and is in us and around us.

Step 34

• •

Trust in the Lord, and do good; dwell in the land, and feed on
His faithfulness. Delight yourself also in the Lord, and He shall
give you the desires of your heart. Commit your way to the
Lord, trust also in Him, and He shall bring it to pass. He shall
bring forth your righteousness as the light, and your justice as
the noonday. Rest in the Lord, and wait patiently for Him.
—Psalm 37:3–7a (NKJV)

We take pleasure in knowing that we are in Christ, and He is Lord
over our lives. We can smile, laugh, and be thrilled that we have been
saved from the pit of hell and are being prepared for heaven.

Our lives are built around faith in God, trusting that He is looking out for us, monitoring our every thought, decision and action
that we take. We are nourished in His presence and take joy in the
personal relationship we have with Jesus Christ.

As we talk to God through prayer, we have an expectation that
He hears us, will answer, and fulfill our requests. We believe and
don't doubt that the Lord knows what we need and is preparing a
way to get it to us. He is a good dad who is looking out for His kids
and wants to make them happy.

So let's listen to Him and work to align our way to the way He
wants us to go. We rest in knowing God has a plan for our lives and
intends to see it fulfilled. We do not get impatient knowing that in
God's best timing, He will bring it to pass as surely as we know the
sun will rise tomorrow.

Step 35

• •

The steps of a good man are ordered by the Lord,
and He delights in his way.
Though he fall, he shall not be utterly cast down;
for the Lord upholds him with His hand.
I have been young, and now am old;
yet I have not seen the righteous forsaken,
nor his descendants begging bread
He is ever merciful, and lends;
and his descendants are blessed.
But the salvation of the righteous is from the Lord;
He is their strength in the time of trouble.
And the Lord shall help them and deliver them.
—Psalm 37:23–26, 39–40a (NKJV)

We are to stay the course of life even when the going is difficult or boring. We watch our steps and do not deviate to the left or the right. We keep to the middle of the road even when the way is not too exciting. We count our blessings and are glad that God is leading us on the straight and narrow way.

When we stumble and fall, God is present and patient to pick us up and dust us off. We get back up and return to the course God has laid out for us and seek the guidance of the Holy Spirit.

We are children of the Lord who are generous and giving of our resources. When there is extra food or clothing, it is given to a soup kitchen or a clothing cottage, which will take our donations. Not all gifts are material; some are smiles and kind words that come forth. The more we bless others the more we are blessed. A generous spirit has been released in us so that we can be givers.

Step 36

● ●

> As the deer pants for the water brooks,
> so pants my soul for You, O God.
> My soul thirsts for God, for the living God.
> Why are you cast down, O my soul?
> And why are you disquieted within me?
> Hope in God, for I shall yet praise Him
> for the help of His countenance.
> —Psalm 42:1–2, 5 (NKJV)

The things of this world are so senseless and foolish; they cause us to desire the things of heaven. The outrage, the causes, the emotion, and the anger are so far from God, and it all seems meaningless and temporary. What we desire are the deeper things of God where true life is found.

So we hunger and thirst after the wisdom and truth reserved in heaven to be released on earth. Our spirit senses those things and connects with them by the Holy Spirit.

We call out to God to bring our thoughts into alignment with Jesus. We ask Him to bring our emotions under control and release peace and joy into us again. We ask the Holy Spirit to strip us of sinful desires and to purify us once more. This brings us back onto the narrow road and keeps us in His care.

There is a hole in our hearts and a longing for more of the Lord. It doesn't look like it sometimes, but nothing fills that void like the presence of God. Only He can satisfy us when the things of the world fall short. We pray for help to keep our attention on what God is saying to us today.

Step 37

• •

God is our refuge and strength, a very present help
in trouble. Therefore, we will not fear,
even though the earth be removed,
and though the mountains be carried into the midst of the sea;
though its waters roar and be troubled,
though the mountains shake with its swelling.
Be still, and know that I am God;
I will be exalted among the nations,
I will be exalted in the earth!
—Psalm 46:1–3, 10 (NKJV)

Natural and manmade disasters are with us every day somewhere in the world. But God is present at the same time with safety and help to all who will call on His name. God is asking if we will turn to Him in the midst of our troubles. We have a choice to go it on our own, refusing His help, rebelling against Him, and not believing He is real. Or we can recognize His gracious help and draw on His strength.

A flood or a fire can destroy all we have accumulated and depend on. Some will escape it with just the clothes on their backs. Man-made shelters are set up, and emergency supplies made available. These are often by the grace of God.

However, a deeper longing and need is at the very core of our being. It requires us to call on God who has promised to be our rescue and hope in the time of need. No matter how difficult the struggle, we are not to fear but to trust Him throughout the bad times.

God is commanding us to be quiet before Him and to know that He is greater than any disaster, and He knows just what we need. It begins with accepting His peace, calming our emotions, letting go of fear, kneeling at His feet, and thanking Him.

Step 38

• •

> Oh, clap your hands, all you peoples! Shout to God with the
> voice of triumph! For the Lord Most High is awesome; He is
> a great King over all the earth. God has gone up with a shout,
> the Lord with the sound of a trumpet. Sing praises to God,
> sing praises! Sing praises to our King, sing praises! For God is
> the King of all the earth; sing praises with understanding.
> —Psalm 47:1–2 (NKJV)

The Lord is great and greatly to be praised. He has triumphed over
His enemies and has gained the victory. He has ascended into heaven
and sits with honor at the right hand of the Father.

We share in the victory He has won over the devil. We died with
Him. We were buried with Him and raised up with Him to new life.
With a voice of praise, we lift Him up and shout His name, Jesus,
Lord of Lords, King of Kings! His name is great over all the earth and
the heavens.

Jesus Christ is coming again before the great tribulation. The
dead in Christ will rise first, and then those in Christ who remain
alive will be taken up with Him and all the saints will sing praises!
This is the "rapture" of the church and those who are left behind
and did not believe in Christ will face the Tribulation and wonder at
where are all the Christians. As they ponder these things when the
world is crashing all around them, they will have one more chance to
give their hearts to the Lord and be saved.

Step 39

• •

Create in me a clean heart, O God, And renew a
steadfast spirit within me. Do not cast me
away from Your presence,
And do not take Your Holy Spirit from me.
Restore to me the joy of Your salvation,
And uphold me by Your generous Spirit.
The sacrifices of God are a broken spirit,
A broken and a contrite heart.
These, O God, You will not despise.
—Psalm 51:10–12, 17 (NKJV)

When we deviate slightly off course, God is there to nudge us back on the narrow path. But if we have fallen away from God, a bigger adjustment is necessary. We don't need CPR but rather a new heart and a new way of thinking. Salvation was not lost, but the spirit was quiet, and the presence of the Lord could not be felt.

So wake us up, Lord, bring us back to You, turn us from our sins, and restore within us a clean heart. God is so patient with us, and just like the prodigal son, He takes us back and revives our joy.

The joy of our salvation brings about a course correction. We remember the ultimate sacrifice that Jesus made for us. It becomes clear once again that the old man is dead, and the new man must take his place. The pleasures of the old lifestyle cannot compare with the presence and leading of the Holy Spirit. We put on a new set of lenses so we can see the great plan that God has for our lives. The Holy Spirit please keeps us strong in the midst of temptation and rebellion to follow our Father and complete the tasks ahead.

Step 40

• •

You number my wanderings; put my tears into
Your bottle; are they not in Your book?
When I cry out to You,
then my enemies will turn back;
this I know, because God is for me.
In God (I will praise His word),
in the Lord (I will praise His word),
in God I have put my trust;
I will not be afraid.
What can man do to me?
For You have delivered my soul from death.
Have You not kept my feet from falling,
that I may walk before God
in the light of the living?
—Psalm 56:8–11, 13 (NKJV)

God knows everything about us, our comings and goings. He is aware of our thoughts, fears, and our disappointments. He is for us in all things, and He hears our cry for help.

Man or the devil cannot bring us down. We have put our full faith and trust in God. As we study it, the Word of God is full of His promises and encouragement for us. When we put our trust in Him, our sorrows and fears fade away. We believe God speaks to us out of the Written Word as we read it, meditate on it, and take it to heart.

We praise and thank God for all He has done for us. He has saved us from the pit of hell. He shines His light upon us so that we do not wander in darkness. He protects us from a fall and sustains us on our journey.

We sense His presence and walk out our days with confidence. If God is for us, and He is, then who can be against us? The enemy better get out of the way because we are a mighty force as we walk with God!

Step 41

● ●

My heart is steadfast, O God, my heart is steadfast; I will sing
and give praise. Awake, my glory! Awake, lute and harp! I will
awaken the dawn. I will praise You, O Lord, among the peoples;
I will sing to You among the nations. For Your mercy reaches
unto the heavens, and Your truth unto the clouds. Be exalted, O
God, above the heavens; let Your glory be above all the earth.
—Psalm 57:7–11 (NKJV)

God is great and greatly to be praised! We will sing praises to Him
because He has done great things. If we don't sing praises to God, then
the rocks and trees will cry out. The trees will wave their branches,
and the rocks will no longer be silent.

Praise and worship to the Lord are weapons against the plot of
the enemy. He hates it when we praise God; he covers his ears and
runs away.

The spirit inside of us is eager to praise. The mind is directed
to think of words of praise. The emotions are stirred by the depth of
God's love for us. The will makes a decision to release praises to God.

Our mouths open, and the song of praise come forth. Each new
day is an opportunity to sing a song to the Lord. And why not? He
is worthy to be praised, honored, and exalted. Where would we be
without the presence and the power of God in our lives? The Son
honors the Father and the Holy Spirit directs us to praise the Son,
Jesus Christ.

So we let the praises come forth. We will not be silent. The Lord
has done great things. Let our lives be anthems of praise and our
mouths be open to shout His name, unending and forever!

Step 42

• •

Hear my cry, O God; Attend to my prayer. From the end of the
earth I will cry to You, When my heart is overwhelmed; Lead
me to the rock that is higher than I. For You have been a shelter
for me, A strong tower from the enemy. I will abide in Your
tabernacle forever; I will trust in the shelter of Your wings.
—Psalm 61:1–4 (NKJV)

In our own strength, we are weak and subject to temptation. We
sometimes forget where our strength lies and the source of it. In
pride, we forget to call out for help, or we reject the rock who is Jesus
Christ our Lord.

We call out to God to draw us to the shelter and strong tower
from the enemy. Without the help of the Lord, we are easily stomped
and kicked into the gutter of life. Our thinking needs shaking to
reason clearly and to see the consequences of poor choices. We need
to step into a new day with a resolve to never leave our shelter of
protection.

The devil and his demons have had his way with us for too
long. We are trusting in the Lord Almighty who is the strong tower
we run to. We will resist him in the next attack with the power of the
Holy Spirit.

The enemy is no match for the power of God, and he cannot defeat us. He might win a little victory over us, but the war has
already been won by Jesus at the cross. Our sins were nailed to that
cross, and we were resurrected into new life with Him.

Step 43

• •

My soul, wait silently for God alone, for my expectation is from
Him. He only is my rock and my salvation; He is my defense; I
shall not be moved. In God is my salvation and my glory; the rock
of my strength, and my refuge, is in God. Trust in Him at all times,
you people; pour out your heart before Him; God is a refuge for us.
—Psalm 62:5–8 (NKJV)

This is a time for well thought out decisions in business and relationships. We are to wait before walking into something that could be
detrimental to us. Let's not be in a hurry before we have heard from
the Lord concerning the situation.

Sometimes we jump to a conclusion before we have all the facts.
We might accuse or criticize needlessly when things will look different after a little more time. God sees all that is before us in a way that
has no human limits. He is available to guide us through the difficulties if we will wait and listen to Him. He knows it's not easy in this
life so He has sent the Holy Spirit to be our guide.

There is a supernatural peace when we wait and trust God
for the right choice. Our flesh wants to rush ahead of God in pride
and overconfidence. Sometimes we think God is moving too slowly
when, in fact, His timing is perfect.

So He is asking us today if we will jump ahead or wait quietly
before Him. When our spirit is lined up with the Holy Spirit, then
there is a peace as we sort through the various options in front of us.
It's a good feeling to know we have made a God-choice!

Step 44

• •

O God, You are my God;
early will I seek You;
my soul thirsts for You;
my flesh longs for You
in a dry and thirsty land
where there is no water.
So I have looked for You in the sanctuary,
to see Your power and Your glory.
Because Your lovingkindness is better than life,
my lips shall praise You.
Thus I will bless You while I live;
I will lift up my hands in Your name.
Because You have been my help,
therefore in the shadow of Your wings I will rejoice.
My soul follows close behind You;
Your right hand upholds me.
—Psalm 63:1–4, 7–8 (NKJV)

Not only are we looking for God, He is seeking after us. Remember how the father of the prodigal son ran to meet him? That is God's desire for us. His loving-kindness soothes the stress and difficulties of this life.

We hunger and thirst after Him, and He satisfies us. Our response to a graceful God is to praise and worship Him. We are to put our full faith and trust in Him.

All our souls' parts are to be committed and connected to Him. We are to leave time in our day for Him. We can't be too busy or tired to seek God in our circumstances. He is our strength, our help, and our safety in all things. He has provided His right arm, Jesus, to travel with us on this life journey.

Step 45

· ·

Make a joyful shout to God, all the earth!Sing
out the honor of His name;
make His praise glorious.
Who keeps our soul among the living,
and does not allow our feet to be moved.
If I regard iniquity in my heart,
the Lord will not hear.
But certainly God has heard me;
He has attended to the voice of my prayer.
—Psalm 66:1–2, 9, 18–19 (NKJV)

Let's praise the name of Jesus from the mountain top to the valley below, all the continents to give a shout of praise and all the islands to sing out honor to His name. Our praises bring glory to the King of kings.

If we doubt that Jesus is Lord, then the Word of God assures us that He has chosen us and keeps us close to Him. We are in the world, but we are not of it. As we venture out into the world, He protects us, and the Holy Spirit is our guide. When the world questions our beliefs, we stand strong and are not moved. The Holy Spirit gives us the words at the right moment to defend Jesus.

The accuser will point to our past sins and remind us of them. But the key point is that they are in the past, covered by the blood of Jesus, and are forgotten. Even if the devil presents our past sins to the Father, He does not see them or hear of them because they are removed by Jesus and buried with our old self. We walk in forgiveness and newness of life. We are not bound by the sins of the past. What an awesome and wonderful God we love and serve.

Step 46

• •

In You, O Lord, I put my trust; let me never be put to shame.
Deliver me in Your righteousness, and cause me to escape; incline
Your ear to me, and save me. Be my strong refuge, to which
I may resort continually; You have given the commandment
to save me, for You are my rock and my fortress. Deliver me,
O my God, out of the hand of the wicked, out of the hand
of the unrighteous and cruel man. For You are my hope, O
Lord God; You are my trust from my youth. By You I have
been upheld from birth; You are He who took me out of my
mother's womb. My praise shall be continually of You.
—Psalm 71:1–6 (NKJV)

The accusations will come; some are true, and others are false. The charges against us are often without merit, untrue, and baseless. For those criticisms, let them fade away and have no impact.

For those that are true, let us repent before God and man and receive correction. There is only one who is perfect; His name is Jesus. As we live and breathe in this world, we will make mistakes. What is important is not to deny them or to ignore them. We have a refuge in the Lord who we continually run to.

God has known us and watched us from our birth. As a good dad, He is continually looking out for us. He is filing off the rough edges of our character and making us more like Jesus each day.

So we thank Him for looking out for us and loving us through the good times and the bad. We praise Him and thank Him for His patience and kindness to us each day. We can put our hope in God and trust Him for our future. Let us work to make each new day better than yesterday. When we are weak, He is strong, and when we are down, He is the source of our joy.

Step 47

• •

Whom have I in heaven but You? And there is none upon
earth that I desire besides You. My flesh and my heart fail;
but God is the strength of my heart and my portion forever.
But it is good for me to draw near to God;
I have put my trust in the Lord God,
that I may declare all Your works.
—Psalm 73:25–26, 28 (NKJV)

There is a whole team of good fighting for us. God is for us, so who
can be against us? Jesus has made a way for us and has come to live
inside of us. The Holy Spirit is helping, guiding, comforting, and
strengthening us in all things. And if that wasn't enough, there are
unseen angels released and sent to protect us.

In the strength of our own heart and flesh, we would give up
and quit. But God's power and presence is more than enough for us.
He is there for us, even when we feel down, alone, and forsaken. The
world and the devil are no match for the powers of heaven.

So we will draw near to God and seek His presence and put our
full faith and trust in Him. What can mere man do to us when we
are in the shadow of the Most High?

When our friends or family are stuck in a difficult situation, we
will pray for them and point them to God. We will declare all the
works of God as long as they will listen.

Step 48

• •

> For a day in Your courts is better than a thousand. I would rather be a doorkeeper in the house of my God than dwell in the tents of wickedness. For the Lord God is a sun and shield; the Lord will give grace and glory; no good thing will He withhold From those who walk uprightly. O Lord of hosts, blessed is the man who trusts in You!
> —Psalm 84:10–12 (NKJV)

A celebration of this earthly life does not compare with the glory of heaven. At the end of this life, we are promised entry into the kingdom of God. And the kingdom is a present reality although not to the degree of the future one. We get to enjoy a taste of heaven now.

It's nearly impossible for us to imagine a future without sin. However, we have been unloaded of the burden of past sins by accepting the works of Jesus Christ at the cross. We have been given the Holy Spirit and His power to keep us out of sin.

The peace of heaven must be wonderful. There is a supernatural peace that is available to us now as we allow Jesus to take our worries and concerns about this life. There is no pain in heaven, and we look forward to a time without it. Salvation includes a health and healing of the body and soul that we can draw on now.

As we walk in the righteousness of God and trust Him through the challenges of this life, we get a foretaste of how good heaven is going to be. Living in the light of God now and counting on a future with Jesus makes all the difference to us.

Step 49

. . . .

I will hear what God the Lord will speak,
for He will speak peace
to His people and to His saints;
but let them not turn back to folly.
Mercy and truth have met together;
righteousness and peace have kissed.
Righteousness will go before Him,
and shall make His footsteps our pathway.
—Psalm 85:8, 10, 13 (NKJV)

The Lord is speaking to our hearts, but we are not always listening. He wants to take us out of strife, discontent, and rebellion into a place of peace and cooperation. We are the blocks and mortar for the kingdom He is building on earth that which will be fully consummated when He returns.

God's mercy gives us more chances to live this life as He desires. He is truth and makes it available to us if we will just be open to it. The truth is God is merciful toward His people and teaches them not to return to the old ways.

Jesus has put us in right standing with the Father. He is happy that we have left the old lifestyle and begun to walk in righteousness. Knowing our right position with God brings a supernatural calmness to our souls.

There is power in knowing who we are in Christ. The devil's grip on our behavior has loosened. The way of the old self is no longer interesting, desirable, or attractive. We sometimes wonder why we didn't leave the old prison of sin and defeat sooner. It is our plan to make the second half of our lives more fulfilling and productive than the first half with the help of the Holy Spirit we will!

Step 50

• •

Teach me Your way, O Lord; I will walk in Your truth;
unite my heart to fear Your name. I will praise You, O
Lord my God, with all my heart, and I will glorify Your
name forevermore. For great is Your mercy toward me, and
You have delivered my soul from the depths of Sheol.
—Psalm 86:11–13 (NKJV)

We have tried living life our own way, and that only leads to the pit of hell. Thank You for rescuing us and showing us a better way. We are not satisfied to know only a little of You. Our desire is for more knowledge and power.

Let our journey into the more of God begin with praise and worship. In praise, there is thanksgiving and wonder at all He has done for us. Thank God that He has taken us from the road of destruction to a new and refreshing way of life. Thank God that He knows what is best for us and is revealing His truth to us in our daily walk with Him.

Lord, help us to pick up the pieces of our life and assemble them into something meaningful. The old worn out sinful desires can be left buried, but the God inspired, creative, and joyful parts can be developed. In this new life, let us be loving, kind, and peace-giving creatures. He knows us and created us in His image to make a difference and to finish out our days in a simple and significant way.

Step 51

● ●

The heavens are Yours, the earth also is Yours; the world and all
its fullness, You have founded them. You have a mighty arm;
strong is Your hand, and high is Your right hand.
Blessed are the people who know the joyful sound!
They walk, O Lord, in the light of Your countenance.
In Your name they rejoice all day long,
and in Your righteousness they are exalted.
—Psalm 89:11, 13, 15–16 (NKJV)

God created the heavens and the earth, and He saw that it was good.
There is not another planet in the galaxy that is conducive for life like
the earth. Even though the devil and man's intentions have spoiled
our dwelling place, we can still see the beauty of our home.

We can take joy because God has sent His Son, Jesus Christ, to
bring salvation and righteousness to anyone who will receive Him
as Lord and Savior. We are blessed in spite of the pain and misery
around us.

As we begin to live like Jesus, we can see the world in a whole
different way. What spoils our world is no religion or false religion.
A belief in God and a life given over to Him is our only hope. A life
without God is devoid of hope, love, joy, peace, and goodness.

A life 100 percent dependent on self is a worship of idols. A
rejection of God creates blindness and a walk in darkness. But Your
people, O Lord, walk in the light, and they sense Your presence. We
have found true purpose of life, and because of it, we have a sense of
joy.

Step 52

• •

Lord, You have been our dwelling place in all generations.
Before the mountains were brought forth,
or ever You had formed the earth and the world,
even from everlasting to everlasting, You are God.
So teach us to number our days,
that we may gain a heart of wisdom.
And let the beauty of the Lord our God be upon us,
and establish the work of our hands for us;
yes, establish the work of our hands.
—Psalm 90:1–2, 12, 17 (NKJV)

God is from the past. He is ever present and forever. He is eternal and has no beginning nor ending. He knew us before we were born and will be with us forever. There is no place that we can hide from Him nor have a desire to. God has given us a lifetime and numbered our days here on earth. What will we do with them? Will we squander them on foolish pursuits or waste them until we are no more?

Father, teach us to value our lives, to make them significant, to seek worth in our time here. Let our thoughts be your thoughts, our emotions to be under control, and our actions pleasing in Your sight. May we grow in the knowledge of You with each passing day and may we desire, seek, and enjoy Your presence.

You have a purpose and a destiny for each of us. Help us to be alert fulfilling Your plan for our lives. May we shine like the noonday sun and delight to do Your bidding. As a child of the Most High God, let us project Your beauty and goodness to those around us. Let the beauty of the Lord be known throughout the earth.

Step 53

● ●

He who dwells in the secret place of the Most High Shall abide under the shadow of the Almighty. I will say of the Lord, "He is my refuge and my fortress; My God, in Him I will trust." Surely He shall deliver you from the snare of the fowler and from the perilous pestilence. He shall cover you with His feathers, and under His wings you shall take refuge; His truth shall be your shield and buckler. You shall not be afraid of the terror by night, nor of the arrow that flies by day, nor of the pestilence that walks in darkness, nor of the destruction that lays waste at noonday.
—Psalm 91:1–6 (NKJV)

We live and dwell in the presence of the Lord. It is there that we feel His safety and the strength to resist the enemy. With our mouths, we declare that Jesus is Lord and God, and in Him, we will trust and be safe.

The enemy comes around and tries to entrap us and keep us from our God. He tries to bring sickness upon us and to steal our good health. He attempts to steal our money and bring us into poverty. Discouragement and futility are his calling cards. But we will have none of it because we have been delivered from the enemy's camp and are covered in the shelter of the Lord.

The truth is God is in charge and in control so we will listen to His instructions and follow His advice. Fear shall not come near us by day or by night. In Christ, there is power, love, and a sound mind. Why would we seek any other lifestyle and believe the devil's lies?

Step 54

• •

> Because you have made the Lord, who is my refuge, even the
> Most High, your dwelling place, no evil shall befall you, nor shall
> any plague come near your dwelling; for He shall give His angels
> charge over you, to keep you in all your ways. In their hands
> they shall bear you up, lest you dash your foot against a stone.
> —Psalm 91:9–12 (NKJV)

We have declared our allegiance and our lives to the Lord our God. In doing so, the forces of heaven have been released in our behalf. The devil no longer has power over us. Sickness, poverty, and discouragement cannot come near to us.

The angelic forces of heaven are in charge of our comings and goings. Even though they are invisible to us, they are directed by God to watch out for us and protect us. No matter where we might travel or what we do, they are present to help us.

Even when we make the wrong choices or are not careful, the angels are there for us. Combine that with the power, guidance, and comfort of the Holy Spirit, and we need not worry or be afraid. No evil thing can get his hands on us or persuade us to be entrapped by it. Our task is to listen and obey the instructions of the Lord.

Step 55

• •

"Because he has set his love upon Me, therefore I will deliver
him; I will set him on high, because he has known My name.
He shall call upon Me, and I will answer him; I will be with
him in trouble; I will deliver him and honor him. With
long life I will satisfy him, and show him My salvation."
—Psalm 91:14–16 (NKJV)

We love our families, our friends, but most importantly, our love is
directed to God. We are instructed to love God, love others and ourselves as well. God has promised to deliver us from whatever is holding us back. He desires to honor us in lives that are dedicated to Him.

Anyone who has given his life to God has an open line of com-
munication with the Father. God desires to talk with us and help us
through our troubles. We must remember to seek Him when the
going gets difficult.

We have been given a lifetime to get our relationship right with
God and to fulfill our calling. We don't know how much time we have,
so there is a sense of urgency to respond quickly. We can do a lot to
extend our lives, eat right, exercise, and maintain a healthy body. God
desires that we care for the body and life that He has given us.

There is only so much we can do before our time runs out and
we go to heaven. Bottom line is long lives and saved lives are by the
grace of God. So we thank Him for this earthly life and look forward
to eternity in heaven.

Step 56

● ●

It is good to give thanks to the Lord,
and to sing praises to Your name, O Most High;
to declare Your lovingkindness in the morning,
and Your faithfulness every night,
for You, Lord, have made me glad through Your work;
I will triumph in the works of Your hands.
O Lord, how great are Your works!
Your thoughts are very deep.
—Psalm 92:1–2, 4–5 (NKJV)

Each new day is an opportunity to thank God and give Him praise all over again. We take a moment to think of all the things we are thankful for and break into a new song to God.

We don't deserve all the loving-kindness that God has poured out on us. It's as if He is waiting for us to wake up so He can shower His love upon us again. We are not always faithful to God and fall short in many ways, but it never seems to affect his faithfulness to us. We shout, "Glory to God in the highest."

You have released a joy in us that we could not find in the world. We look inside of us, and there You are, and we look around us, and there You are too! So we resolve to make You a proud dad as we go about our daily activities.

How great are Your works, O Lord, we marvel at them. And yet it seems we only know You on a Sunday school level. Take us deeper in our knowledge of You so that we might know You better in a private and personal way.

Step 57

● ●

The righteous shall flourish like a palm tree, He shall grow like a cedar in Lebanon. Those who are planted in the house of the Lord shall flourish in the courts of our God. They shall still bear fruit in old age; they shall be fresh and flourishing, to declare that the Lord is upright; He is my rock, and there is no unrighteousness in Him.
—Psalm 92:12–15 (NKJV)

We are strong and flourishing because we have given our lives to the Lord. It might not seem so on the outside, but we have an inner strength that will carry us through till the end. We are on a journey in this life, and those who are successful are the ones whose lives are given over to the Lord.

The object of this life is to bear fruit for the Lord on a daily basis. What can we do with the time that we have been given to contribute and give back? There is more to life than breathing and taking up space. What is the Lord calling us to do?

Even though our minds might fail and our bodies become weak, we will declare that "Jesus is Lord." To stand in His presence is to be strong and step up to the next challenge. So that is our prayer today that we will be planted securely in the house of the Lord. Let us be fresh and flourishing in the Lord and bearing fruit even in our old age.

We declare that "Jesus is our rock." In Him is no unrighteousness and, therefore, none in us. Because He is solid and eternal, we align ourselves with Him and share in His righteousness.

Step 58

He who planted the ear, shall He not hear? He who formed
the eye, shall He not see? He who instructs the nations, shall
He not correct, He who teaches man knowledge? The Lord
knows the thoughts of man, that they are futile. Blessed is the
man whom You instruct, O Lord, and teach out of Your law.
—Psalm 94:9–12 (NKJV)

When we consider the creation, we realize that God is the author
and the artist of all life. We marvel at our abilities to see, hear, smell,
taste, and feel. Our bodies are amazing machines designed by the
great Creator God. To imagine mankind evolved out of the slime on
a planet that just happened to appear over billions of years ago is just
silly foolishness.

We appreciate worldly knowledge taught in our schools, but
it does not compare with the wisdom of God. However, God plus
schooling is a powerful force in the world today. When we allow God
to direct our education, we are way ahead in the game of life.

God, who created our brains and mental capacities, knows our
every thought. God knows all we need to move on in this life.

We are not alone in the struggles and challenges of life. When
we allow God to instruct us, blessings begin to emerge for us. Our
thoughts are not His thoughts, but God desires to share His thoughts.
With just a fraction of His secrets and His wisdom with us, we are
well equipped to face the future. We have a plan for us, and God has
one. Which one is better is an easy choice.

Step 59

Unless the Lord had been my help, my soul would soon
have settled in silence. If I say, "My foot slips," Your mercy,
O Lord, will hold me up. In the multitude of my anxieties
within me, Your comforts delight my soul. But the Lord has
been my defense, and my God the rock of my refuge.
—Psalm 94:17–19, 22 (NKJV)

Lord, we thank You for rescuing us with Your salvation from certain disaster. If God hadn't reached out for us and gathered us in, we would have reaped an eternity of regret.

Daily we need God's care and protection to keep our bodies free from sickness and injury. We call out in the midst of our pain, and He is there to soothe us.

Worry sneaks up on us when we least expect it. Jesus said, "Do not worry," and yet we sometimes forget the command. We know that worry doesn't fix anything, just makes it worse, no matter how much time we spend in it. Thank God, He delivered us from worry and fear. God helps us to replace those emotions with His confidence, trust, and comfort.

The shield of faith is our defense against the arrows of fear and doubt. We are in a spiritual battle; God helps us to use all the defensive weapons of our warfare and to defeat the enemy who comes against us. When things get too difficult to bear, we run to the Lord who is our strong tower of protection. There we cling to the rock of refuge who is Jesus Christ, our Lord.

Step 60

●●●●●●●●●●●●●●●●●●●●●●●●●●●●●●●●●●

Oh come, let us sing to the Lord!
Let us shout joyfully to the rock of our salvation.
Let us come before His presence with thanksgiving;
let us shout joyfully to Him with psalms.
For the Lord is the great God,
and the great King above all gods.
Oh come let us worship and bow down;
let us kneel before the Lord our Maker.
For He is our God,
and we are the people of His pasture,
and the sheep of His hand.
—Psalm 95:1–3, 6–7 (NKJV)

God always was and always will be. Great men and women have come and gone. Memories of them will fade with each new generation. But God will be honored forever, people will sing praises, shouts will go up, and new songs will be song.

We are standing in the midst of greatness when we stand in the presence of our Lord. He always deserves our praises and thanksgiving.

Jesus Christ is the rock of our salvation, and to Him, we sing and shout our praises. He reigns as King in the hearts of believers today. He will be recognized at the second coming, and He will rule on earth for one thousand years.

God is delighted when Jesus is the topic of our conversation. He is proud when hymns and songs of praise exalt Him in worship services. He is encouraging us to share what Jesus has done through preaching, writing, and singing. What a privilege to know that we are His people, and He is our God. Its reason is enough for us to shout halleluiah and to fall on our knees in prayer. We are people of praise and worship for Jesus, so let's release it today!

Step 61

Oh, sing to the Lord a new song! Sing to the Lord, all
the earth. Sing to the Lord, bless His name; proclaim
the good news of His salvation from day to day.
Declare His glory among the nations,
His wonders among all peoples.
For the Lord is great and greatly to be praised;
He is to be feared above all gods.
Honor and majesty are before Him;
strength and beauty are in His sanctuary.
—Psalm 96:1–4, 6 (NKJV)

Each new day is an opportunity to sing praises to the Lord. Each new season and year brings chances to proclaim the salvation of the Lord. With each new job or project, we can declare the glory and wonders of the Lord.

Spring is especially a time to break out in song in the midst of wildflowers, green grass, trees, and the warming of the sun. It is all a reminder that there is strength and beauty in His presence.

We can only imagine the chorus of praise that goes up to the Lord every day. It certainly drowns out the curses that are spoken against God. So come let us bow down before the Lord. Let's bring an offering of songs, tithes, words of wisdom, and service to the holy of holies.

I pray for a mighty move of the Holy Spirit across the land that will draw people to the Lord. May the unrighteous know that they live in a cursed world and under the power of sin. Open their eyes, Lord, to see the error of their ways and to repent. Time is short. Jesus could return at any time, and we need to be ready to meet Him.

Step 62

● ●

Let the heavens rejoice, and let the earth be glad; let the sea roar, and all its fullness; let the field be joyful, and all that is in it. Then all the trees of the woods will rejoice before the Lord. For He is coming, for He is coming to judge the earth. He shall judge the world with righteousness, and the peoples with His truth.
—Psalm 96:11–13 (NKJV)

God the Creator has established the heavens and the earth. Let us rejoice and be glad in it. He has made the seas and filled them with water. He established the lands and covered them with the plants and animals. We join with all creation to honor and exalt the Almighty God.

God's prize creation was mankind, made in His own image. He allowed a devil to tempt and entice us out of a perfect environment and relationship with our heavenly Father. He sent His Son, Jesus, to make a way for us to regain that special and powerful relationship with Him.

We have been given this life to repent of our sins, receive our forgiveness, fulfill a plan, and complete a calling for our lives. This is the time to realize our righteousness and live it out in thanksgiving to Jesus.

The Lord Jesus is coming back to judge the living and the dead. The disciples and Paul anticipated His return and taught us to be ready. Because we have already been judged righteous, we can move on into eternity with joy. The Word of God is truth, there is no error in it, and so we can trust it and be at peace.

Step 63

• •

You who love the Lord, hate evil! He preserves the souls
of His saints; He delivers them out of the hand of the
wicked. Light is sown for the righteous, and gladness for
the upright in heart. Rejoice in the Lord, you righteous,
and give thanks at the remembrance of His holy name.
—Psalm 97:10–12 (NKJV)

We are in a battle for our lives, but it is not a physical one. It is a
spiritual battle for our minds, emotions, and decision-making. The
enemy is sly; he will attack our weaknesses and attempt to knock us
off course with tactics that have worked before.

By the power of the Holy Spirit, our souls are preserved and
protected. Jesus defeated the devil at the cross of Calvary. We have
been delivered from and separated from the enemy's camp. We must
pray for our friends and family that are still in darkness.

We are the righteousness of the Lord, and we walk in the light
of His revelation and wisdom. We rejoice in our salvation and calling
from the Lord. We walk in the light as He is in the light. His Word
enlightens us as He reveals a path laid out for us.

There is an inner joy and gladness that only comes from walking in the light. We are thankful to the Lord for the gift of new life
and hope that is supernatural. Our hearts and minds are joined to the
Lord to experience and exercise all that He has for us. We reverence
and honor His holy name.

Step 64

● ●

> Oh, sing to the Lord a new song! For He has done marvelous things; His right hand and His holy arm have gained Him the victory. The Lord has made known His salvation; His righteousness He has revealed in the sight of the nations. He has remembered His mercy and His faithfulness to the house of Israel; all the ends of the earth have seen the salvation of our God. Shout joyfully to the Lord, all the earth; break forth in song, rejoice, and sing praises.
> —Psalm 98:1–4 (NKJV)

What a wonderful plan God has for mankind! Who could have imagined He would send His Son, Jesus, to rescue us and gain victory over sin and the enemy? The devil was even fooled by it, thinking he had stopped the plan at the cross.

What a wonderful Lord and Savior we have in Jesus Christ. What love He showed for us by taking all our sins and laying down His life for us. He became the ultimate sacrifice in obedience to the Father. Because of God's plan, we have forgiveness for all our sins and new life in Christ. And the Holy Spirit has come to remind us and to enforce the plan.

So we do break out in songs of praise and thanksgiving. We realize this plan for our lives is a gift from God. It is by His grace and mercy that we live and have our being. We are the righteousness of God and His children.

What is even more powerful is that Jesus has made salvation available to all who will say yes and accept Him as Lord and Savior. It is a free gift that needs to be opened and enjoyed. This is the way to live this life in power, humility, and thankfulness because He is with us.

Step 65

• •

Make a joyful shout to the Lord, all you lands! Serve the Lord
with gladness; come before His presence with singing. Know
that the Lord, He is God; it is He who has made us, and not
we ourselves; we are His people and the sheep of His pasture.
—Psalm 100:1–3 (NKJV)

What a privilege and an honor to serve the Lord in some capacity
from small to large. Some have served Him from full-time ministry
to smaller acts of kindness. Servant hood stretches from a smile to a
full-time missionary life.

All acts of love and kindness in the name of the Lord are appreciated and recorded. It's not about how much or how great the act
but about faithfulness. What God is asking us for is to use our gifts
for His glory. God is not evaluating us on a scale of one to hundred
but sees them the same. It's not one point for a smile and hundred
points for a finely crafted sermon or a well-written book.

We will know we are on the right track as we come to know our
God better. His desire for our own lives supersedes our own desires.
He is the One who has equipped us with a unique set of skills and
abilities. What He has placed inside of us is to be used for His honor
and glory.

We can decide what's best to do for the Lord or we can wait
upon Him. He knows where we fit into the larger plan for His kingdom. It's time for us to let go and let God have His way, which of
course is the best way!

Step 66

We are His people and the sheep of His pasture. Enter into His
gates with thanksgiving, and into His courts with praise. Be
thankful to Him, and bless His name. For the Lord is good; his
mercy is everlasting, and His truth endures to all generations.
—Psalm 100:3–5 (NKJV)

When Jesus died on the cross, the veil that covered the door to the
inner court was torn from top to bottom. The Ark of the Covenant
and all the instruments were suddenly in full view. Symbolically, a
way to the throne room of God was opened, and a new way to the
Father was made available.

Now we are able to come into the presence of God, enter into
His gates, and into His courts with praise. All followers of Jesus can
come before the Father directly with praise, worship, and thanksgiving. This was something new that had been closed off from temple
worshippers. The blessings and goodness of God could be experienced in a brand-new way, thanks to Jesus Christ.

It's as if God is saying, "I am good, eternal, and truthful; come
see for yourself." We can bring our requests in the name of Jesus who
sits at the right hand of the Father. We have an intimacy and mercy
with the almighty God of the universe that no other religion can
match.

The truth is His kingdom has come to earth, and His family is
growing. We can come to know the Father of Lights in a whole new
way. We can feel His love and concern for us as never before. We put
our full faith and trust in God who is real and present.

Step 67

• •

Bless the Lord, O my soul, and forget not all His benefits:
who forgives all your iniquities, who heals all your diseases,
who redeems your life from destruction, who crowns you with
lovingkindness and tender mercies, who satisfies your mouth
with good things, so that your youth is renewed like the eagle's.
—Psalm 103:2–5 (NKJV)

Let nothing hold us back from praising the Lord with our whole being. We raise the name of the Lord above ourselves, our homes, and our town. We do that because we remember all He has done for us.

We know within our hearts that God has forgiven all our sins. We are free from the burden and guilt of all our iniquities. Although our sins are many, Jesus has taken them all. We can get up in the morning knowing that our past has been forgiven. The past reminds us of how far we have come and how good our God is.

We thank Him for healing all our sicknesses and diseases. He has taken care of diseases and sins we didn't even know we had. God is sustaining us through difficulties, temptations, and sins that could end our lives. We are in His care and His protection.

He does all this because of His loving kindness and His tender mercies. He makes sure that all our needs are met and that we do not go hungry. He does all these things because we are special in His sight and new creations in Christ Jesus. Wrinkles may come, gray hair, and weariness, but we can say with confidence that our youth is being renewed like the eagles.

Step 68

• •

The Lord is merciful and gracious, slow to anger, and abounding
in mercy. He will not always strive with us, nor will He keep
His anger forever. He has not dealt with us according to
our sins, nor punished us according to our iniquities. For as
the heavens are high above the earth, so great is His mercy
toward those who fear Him; as far as the east is from the
west, so far has He removed our transgressions from us.
—Psalm 103:8–12 (NKJV)

The Lord is merciful and gracious to us. He has withheld punishment from us for our many sins and yet blesses us with blessings we
do not deserve.

Lord, help us to be slow to anger just as You are. We have
become angry with those who come against us and slow to forgive
and forget their behavior. Help us to be more like You and remove
the strife that sneaks into our lives.

Jesus has taken all our sins, and God has withheld the punishment we deserved. Our sins are removed as far as the east is from
the west. Let us not continue in sin thinking there are no consequences for our wrong behavior. Holy Spirit with His mighty power
has delivered us from anything that would keep us from walking in
the true light.

Step 69

As for man, his days are like grass; as a flower of the field, so
he flourishes. For the wind passes over it, and it is gone, and
its place remembers it no more. But the mercy of the Lord is
from everlasting to everlasting on those who fear Him, and His
righteousness to children's children, to such as keep His covenant,
and to those who remember His commandments to do them.
—Psalm 103:15–18

We are like grass that greens up quickly in the springtime, and we
are like wildflowers that grow up, blossom, and mature. But our time
passes quickly, and we grow old before we know it. We finish this life
and leave the faintest mark signifying that we were here.

For those fortunate to have children, a legacy is passed on
through them. By the mercies of God, we transition to the next life
to be with our Lord forever. Hopefully, we have set a good example to
keep His Word and to follow it. Thankfully, we leave this life happy
that the Lord knew us and made us righteous.

We all know we could have used the time we had on earth better. We do the best we can with the days given to us. Hopefully, we
have grown more like Jesus with each passing day. God's grace and
mercy has always been available to us.

So we are thankful for this opportunity to experience His presence and His love in the present. We know our home in heaven will
be grand and glorious. Let our passing be modest and peaceful as we
look forward to the adventure ahead.

Step 70

• •

The Lord has established His throne in heaven, and His
kingdom rules over all. Bless the Lord, you His angels, who
excel in strength, who do His word, Heeding the voice of
His word. Bless the Lord, all you His hosts, You ministers of
His, who do His pleasure. Bless the Lord, all His works, in
all places of His dominion. Bless the Lord, O my soul!
—Psalm 103:19–22 (NKJV)

There is a devil that runs about the earth causing misery and may-
hem. He has an attraction to souls to lead them astray and away from
God. His agenda is to steal, kill, and destroy all flesh.

But God has established His kingdom over the heavens and the
earth. He sees what the devil does and has already judged him and
sentenced him to the lake of fire for eternity. His future is terrible,
and yet he draws ignorant souls to himself.

However, there is a remnant of loving, God-fearing people who
are establishing God's kingdom on earth. They are the ministers of
God speaking truth and living righteously. They are the ones who
delight in carrying out God's instructions.

What a privilege to serve the Lord as His church. We are made
up of pastors, leaders, and lay people who preach the Word, teach
the saints, draw in unbelievers, build God's kingdom, and bring the
prophetic. With all the gifts God has placed in His people, we are
to reveal the word, heal the sick, set free all those who have been
deceived, imprisoned and under the bondages of the devil. We are
to do all these things until Jesus returns and the church is raptured.

Step 71

• •

> May the glory of the Lord endure forever; may the Lord
> rejoice in His works. I will sing to the Lord as long as I live;
> I will sing praise to my God while I have my being. May my
> meditation be sweet to Him; I will be glad in the Lord.
> —Psalm 104:31, 33–34 (NKJV)

We look about us, and we see the works of the Lord that will last forever. Man's accomplishments are temporary and fleeting even though his works are laid upon the Lord's foundation. We are those who are awake to the fact that life is not about us, but the glory and praises are due to God.

So let us sing a song of praise with our whole beings to the Lord. It is He who has made us and not we ourselves. How wonderful and peaceful it is to dwell on all the Lord has done. We meditate on His works, and it brings joy to our hearts.

Our lives have meaning and purpose because they are based on God's foundations. Our thoughts are focused on the eternal thinking of the Lord. We bring our thoughts into submission and let the Holy Spirit have control.

Our emotions are put in check so that anger and sadness are in the background. Let joy and gladness be a sweet offering unto the Lord and may every decision be guided by our close relationship to Jesus.

Step 72

• •

Oh, give thanks to the Lord! Call upon His name; make known His deeds among the peoples! Sing to Him, sing psalms to Him; talk of all His wondrous works! Glory in His holy name; let the hearts of those rejoice who seek the Lord! Seek the Lord and His strength; seek His face evermore! Remember His marvelous works which He has done, His wonders, and the judgments of His mouth.
—Psalm 105:1–5 (NKJV)

Let us give thanks to the Lord and praise Him for His wondrous works. Let there be songs of praise on our lips for His marvelous works. We are products of His amazing grace and creative power.

We will look for opportunities to share our joy and bring glory to His name. We all have testimonies small and large to the miracle working power of the Lord. Today there is someone who needs to hear of the goodness of the Lord from our experience.

As long as we are able, we will seek the Lord for His wisdom and direction for our lives. His plan for us unfolds each day as we keep our eyes upon the Lord. We need His strength to carry out the tasks He has set before us and need His help to overcome the barriers the enemy has set in the path that God has shown us.

Joy, wonder, and praise illuminate our way as we give God the glory in all things. We would have failed if it were not for the Lord's help.

Step 73

Then they cry out to the Lord in their trouble, and He brings
them out of their distresses. He calms the storm, so that its waves
are still. Then they are glad because they are quiet; so He guides
them to their desired haven. Oh, that men would give thanks
to the Lord for His goodness, and for His wonderful works to
the children of men! Let them exalt Him also in the assembly
of the people, and praise Him in the company of the elders.
—Psalm 107:28–32 (NKJV)

The Lord hears us when we cry out to Him in our trouble. He leads
us through our distresses and brings us to the other side. He calms
the storms and shows us a place of safety and peace. He delivers us
out of darkness and replaces it with His marvelous light. Jesus has
healed us and saved us from all our afflictions.

The Lord knows what we are going through and is there to
comfort us. We praise Him for His goodness and wonderful works.
It's only with His presence that we experience a supernatural joy. He
heals our sicknesses and prospers us in our needs.

Oh, that we might see the blessings of the Lord. Even though
He does not take away our troubles, He leads us through them. And
only on the other side do we realize we are stronger and can go on.
He does not leave us without hope. Jesus endured much more than
we can imagine, and He understands the pain of a difficult situation.

Step 74

O God, my heart is steadfast; I will sing and give praise,
even with my glory. I will praise You, O Lord, among the
peoples, and I will sing praises to You among the nations.
For Your mercy is great above the heavens, and Your truth
reaches to the clouds. Be exalted, O God, above the heavens,
and Your glory above all the earth; that Your beloved may
be delivered, save with Your right hand, and hear me.
—Psalm 108:1, 2–6 (NKJV)

Our hearts are steadfast in the Lord. We will not participate in the plans of the enemy. We will sing praises to the Lord at every opportunity and to whoever will listen. Our God is worthy to be praised, morning, noon, and night. Who will tell the people that the Lord is good if we keep silent? There is a truth that comes from God that few know and appreciate. Grace and mercy belong to Him, and He exercises them daily toward His people. We thank the Lord that He has withheld the punishment we deserved and instead poured out His love to us.

Our hearts are steadfast in the Lord; we will not be moved or shaken off of our dependence upon Him. He is the rock on which we stand and the strong tower that we run to which protects us from danger.

Jesus has provided a foundation for our lives. We build on what He has started and brick by brick the kingdom rises up on earth. He has saved a segment of the population in which to construct His church. We are the group that is rescued and washed clean in His blood. If we appear strong and full of joy, it's because of Jesus inside of us, and we are in Him.

Step 75

Praise the Lord! I will praise the Lord with my whole heart, in the
assembly of the upright and in the congregation. The works of
the Lord are great, studied by all who have pleasure in them. His
work is honorable and glorious, and His righteousness endures
forever. He has made His wonderful works to be remembered;
the Lord is gracious and full of compassion. He has given food to
those who fear Him; He will ever be mindful of His covenant.
—Psalm 111:1–5 (NKJV)

We are those who praise and worship the Lord without reservation.
Let all the churches lift up their voices and express their joy and
appreciation for what the Lord is doing in their midst. Let us lead a
procession of praise that stirs the audience and expresses a condition
of the heart.

God has done great things beginning with the warming of the
hardest of hearts. He offers a present blessing followed by a glorious
future of blessings. Why should we be satisfied with the offerings of
the world when there is so much more in the kingdom? Let us seek
those things that are lasting and eternal.

His covenant with the people on earth is in effect until the end
of the age. God's promises are sure, and His truthfulness lasts forever.
He has provided for all of us because of His grace and compassion.

So we look to the Lord and see that He has everything. We need
not be afraid of the darkness but walk completely in the light. He has
provided life and healing to all who will seek Him.

Step 76

● ●

The works of His hands are verity and justice; All His
precepts are sure. They stand fast forever and ever, And are
done in truth and uprightness. He has sent redemption
to His people; He has commanded His covenant forever:
Holy and awesome is His name. The fear of the Lord is the
beginning of wisdom; A good understanding have all those
who do His commandments. His praise endures forever.
—Psalm 111:7–10 (NKJV)

Jesus only said and did what the Father instructed. It kept Him out
of sin and on the plan for His earthly life. He also knew that His
obedience and trust was pleasing to the Father. He followed the way
of truth and the precepts of the Father. He must have known the plan
for His life was not His own and would be different from the rest
of mankind. It had to be or He could not have fulfilled the mission
of drawing people to Himself and offering the gift of salvation to
mankind.

Jesus Christ set the bar high for any that would follow Him.
We know that only by following Jesus can we get a glimpse of eternal
wisdom. We are those who have given our lives over to Jesus, received
the gift of salvation, and been made righteous. And having made that
decision, we cannot return to the old lifestyle, but we press into more
of what God has for us. What a privilege to be a disciple of Jesus and
have the opportunity to live in His light. All praise and honor to the
Son of God!

Step 77

• •

Praise the Lord! Blessed is the man who fears the Lord, who
delights greatly in His commandments. His descendants will be
mighty on earth; the generation of the upright will be blessed.
Wealth and riches will be in his house, and his righteousness
endures forever. Unto the upright there arises light in the
darkness; He is gracious, and full of compassion, and righteous.
A good man deals graciously and lends; He will guide his affairs
with discretion. Surely he will never be shaken; the righteous
will be in everlasting remembrance. He will not be afraid of
evil tidings; His heart is steadfast, trusting in the Lord.
—Psalm 112:1–7 (NKJV)

What a joy it is to know that God has written to us a love letter
through His Word. It comes with instructions on how to live this
life. And it's the account of Jesus, His Son, who loved us and gave
His life for us.

In Christ, we have salvation and righteousness that lasts forever.
Our children raised in a Christian home have a head start toward a
blessed life. We have access to wealth and riches in this life from God
who created all things and sustains them through Christ.

We are the people of God's kingdom who walk in the light that
displaces darkness. We are people of grace exhibiting God's loving
kindness and His righteousness. We live not for ourselves but in the
presence of Christ and give generously to the work of ministry and to
the poor. We will manage our finances carefully and with the wisdom
of the Holy Spirit. When the world's economic system is shaky our
affairs are on solid ground. We will not be afraid of bad news because
in Christ, we have good news our hearts are established, committed
to the Lord, and trusting Him in all things.

Step 78

● ●

> Blessed be the name of the Lord from this time forth and forevermore! From the rising of the sun to its going down the Lord's name is to be praised. The Lord is high above all nations, His glory above the heavens. Who is like the Lord our God, who dwells on high, who humbles Himself to behold the things that are in the heavens and in the earth?
> —Psalm 113:2–6 (NKJV)

If the people of God don't praise Him, then will the rocks cry out and the trees wave their branches instead? We will praise the name of the Lord from morning till night. There is power in praise and worship that cleanses the soul.

We cannot imagine how the almighty God of the universe who created the heavens and the earth cares about each one of us. But He does, listening to every word spoken and aware of every thought that we have. What a relief to know the Creator didn't just put all of this in motion and then distance Himself from His creation. He is very much present and aware of our needs and concerns. He answers our prayers by equipping us to get through each problem with His supernatural strength and wisdom.

The Holy Spirit is the One who is watching out for us and ready to help and comfort us. God's angels are poised to respond to the call for help. The Word of God is living and powerful and contains God's wisdom for us to draw on. The Holy Spirit directs us to passages in the Word that are just what we need in each situation.

Step 79

· ·

I love the Lord, because He has heard
my voice and my supplications.
Because He has inclined His ear to me,
therefore I will call upon Him as long as I live.
Gracious is the Lord, and righteous;
yes, our God is merciful.
Return to your rest, O my soul,
for the Lord has dealt bountifully with you.
For You have delivered my soul from death,
my eyes from tears,
and my feet from falling.
I will walk before the Lord
In the land of the living.
—Psalm 116:1–2, 5, 7–9 (NKJV)

We are so fortunate that God hears our cries out to Him in time of need and danger. We live in a world that promises success and comfort but ultimately can't deliver and can't be trusted. That is because the devil is out to pull us away from God and derail our efforts.

But God has heard our prayers and preserved our lives. The Holy Spirit is leading us through the most difficult of times. Each problem we face is a test to see if we will trust God through it and grow stronger in the midst of trouble.

So we are to believe God's hand is upon us, and He will get us through. Worry and doubt are the enemies in each difficult situation. Instead we are to be at peace knowing that God will provide for us and our children no matter how the future looks.

God is gracious, righteous, and merciful to us, and He is developing the same qualities in us as we walk before Him. This life is a proving ground, and each day offers a challenge to grow stronger in the Lord. The Lord sees our sorrow and stumbling, but He will dry our tears and keep us from falling.

Step 80

● ●

Open to me the gates of righteousness; I will go through them,
and I will praise the Lord. This is the gate of the Lord, through
which the righteous shall enter. I will praise You, for You have
answered me, and have become my salvation. The stone which
the builders rejected has become the chief cornerstone. This
was the Lord's doing; it is marvelous in our eyes. This is the
day the Lord has made; we will rejoice and be glad in it.
—Psalm 118:19–24 (NKJV)

Jesus paid a huge price to accept the lost and found into His kingdom. He was rejected by His own people but did not stop there
instead He turned to the gentiles and made a way for them to be
saved. What grave mistake it is to refuse the Son of God and the gift
of salvation.

As long as one is breathing and can see the love of Jesus for
them, it is not too late. Even in the later days of life, the invitation
and blessing is available to the lost. What patience and mercy God
has for His people, forgiving their sins and cleansing them of all
unrighteousness.

What a blessing to be given long life and length of days! The
Holy Spirit will help us to make the most of each day we are given.
Life passes by quickly, and it is fragile, so we must be active and serv-
ing the Lord while we are able. As long as we have clear heads and
a strong voice, we will praise the Lord. This is the day the Lord has
made. We will be glad in it.

Step 81

Blessed are the undefiled in the way, who walk in the law of the Lord! Blessed are those who keep His testimonies, who seek Him with the whole heart! They also do no iniquity; they walk in His ways. You have commanded us to keep Your precepts diligently. Oh, that my ways were directed to keep Your statutes!
—Psalm 119:1–5 (NKJV)

How will we keep ourselves clean and undefiled? By walking according to God's Word which contains all the instructions and guidelines we need. It's not enough to just read them, scan them, or skip over them. They must be studied and understood deeply. This is different from reading the newspaper or a novel. We are to memorize certain passages and to refer to them in prayer. The better we know them the more likely we are to remember them in time of need.

Once we know some of the Word of God, then we are able to apply it. The Word has the power to keep us in His ways and out of sin. But we need the help of the Holy Spirit bringing the Word to our remembrances. He will bring up the right passage of scripture to fit the present situation. That supernatural help is vital to keeping us on the right path.

We are not ashamed of the Word because we know it comes from God. And we are not embarrassed because we are weak and need to refer to His Word. It's just another way God shows His love for us and equips us to do His work.

Step 82

● ●

> How can a young man cleanse his way?
> By taking heed according to Your word.
> With my whole heart I have sought You;
> oh, let me not wander from Your commandments!
> Your word I have hidden in my heart,
> that I might not sin against You.
> Blessed are You, O Lord!
> Teach me Your statutes.
> I will meditate on Your precepts,
> and contemplate Your ways.
> I will delight myself in Your statutes;
> I will not forget Your word.
> —Psalm 119:9–12, 15–16 (NKJV)

How do we stay out of sin against the Lord? By immersing ourselves in the Word because the more we can know our Bible, the more we can push out the dark thoughts from our minds. The more we line up with God's thoughts, there is less opportunity for the enemy to influence our thoughts. We find God's thoughts and ideas are apparent and revealed in His Word.

Knowing God's Word is not enough, we have to put into action His instructions and apply them to our daily situations. The Bible tells us that faith without works is unproductive, and the same could be said about the Word. We can be a storehouse of scripture verses, but if they are not exercised, then they aren't much good and become stale.

Sometimes we don't need more Word but just to use what we already have stored in our memory. The Word of God is valuable like precious gems, and the task before us is to delight ourselves in it. There is strength in the Word, and it can fuel us on our journey in this life.

Step 83

● ●

My soul clings to the dust;
Revive me according to Your word.
I have declared my ways, and You answered me; Teach me Your
statutes. Make me understand the way of Your precepts;
So shall I meditate on Your wonderful works.
My soul melts from heaviness;
Strengthen me according to Your word.
I will run the course of Your commandments,
For You shall enlarge my heart.
—Psalm 119:25–28, 32 (NKJV)

We desire large hearts for the lost, the downtrodden, and the discouraged. We want to see life through a new lens as God sees it. We have to take the focus off of ourselves and put it on those around us. Let us meditate on God's wonderful works and not on our own.

The cares of this world seem like such a burden at times with no way out. But the Word of the Lord is there for us, ready to strengthen us in our time of need. It makes us understand the Lord's precepts and teaches us to put them to good use.

The Word revives us so that we don't crumble under the pressure of this life. All the education and experience from life does not adequately prepare us for all the challenges put before us. It is only by consulting the Holy Spirit and drawing out the wisdom of the Word that equips us to go on.

The Lord has given us all we need to be productive and successful in this life. Armed with the Word, we are soldiers for Christ that can make a positive difference in this world. We give glory and praise to the name of the Lord.

Step 84

● ●

Teach me, O Lord, the way of Your statutes, And I shall keep it
to the end. Give me understanding, and I shall keep Your law;
Indeed, I shall observe it with my whole heart. Make me walk in
the path of Your commandments, For I delight in it. Incline my
heart to Your testimonies, And not to covetousness. Turn away my
eyes from looking at worthless things, And revive me in Your way.
Establish Your word to Your servant, Who is devoted to fearing You.
—Psalm 119:33–38 (NKJV)

Our desire is to be eager students of the Word of God. It can sustain us all the days of our lives. We will understand it deep within
our hearts, so it is like a well that we can draw from when we are
thirsty. Jesus said that He provides living water for us when we need
it. When we study the Word, our thirst is being satisfied.

Our attitudes have to change so that we don't see the Word
as dull or boring. When we read the Word of God, we are able to
delight in it. Then we can walk guided and directed by the commandments. We turn our eyes from the distractions of the world
because all that glitters are not gold. May the life giving Word be our
desire and attraction.

God's Word brings us new life and makes each day worth getting up for. Sometimes when we study it, the essence and meaning
slips from our consciousness. So when we read it, we will concentrate
and let the Word rule the moment. We will draw on its peace and
power and let it be established it in our hearts.

Step 85

● ●

And I will walk at liberty, For I seek Your precepts. I will speak
of Your testimonies also before kings, And will not be ashamed.
And I will delight myself in Your commandments, Which I
love. My hands also I will lift up to Your commandments,
Which I love And I will meditate on Your statutes.
—Psalm 119:45–48 (NKJV)

We enjoy the mercies of God and are thankful for our salvation. We
know God's Word is the truth we hope in and trust. It gives us an
answer to those critics that question the hope that resides in us.

There is freedom in knowing our place is secure in the kingdom
because of what Jesus has done for us. It's a relief to know deep in our
hearts that we are saved from eternal destruction and darkness.

So we will walk out our freedom because of the love Jesus has
shown us. We don't have to work for our salvation; it is a free gift. We
lift up our hands in praise to the Lord.

The Word of God shows us how to be saved and assures us of
the ultimate sacrifice Jesus made for us. Quite simply it's believing
in our hearts that "Jesus is Lord" and speaking it with our mouths.

We are not ashamed of the Word, but we delight in its commandments. They are not all easy to follow, but we will study and
meditate on them until they are automatic in our behavior.

Step 86

• •

This is my comfort in my affliction, For Your word
has given me life. You are my portion, O Lord; I
have said that I would keep Your words.
I thought about my ways,
And turned my feet to Your testimonies.
I am a companion of all who fear You,
And of those who keep Your precepts.
Teach me good judgment and knowledge,
For I believe Your commandments.
The law of Your mouth is better to me
Than thousands of coins of gold and silver.
—Psalm 119:50, 57, 59, 63, 66, 72 (NKJV)

The only true life we have is in our personal relationship with God.
He comforts us in our afflictions and heals our diseases. God's Word
comforts us and gives us hope.

Before we knew the Lord, our lives were out of control. But
when we turned to Him, things began to change, and we saw ourselves and others in a whole new light. Now we seek His wisdom and
guidance to live each day in a better way.

We have a better understanding and empathy for what others
are going through. It's by taking the focus off of self that we are available to serve others. What a joy it is to worship and spend time with
like-minded believers. Now we see others not just on the surface but
deeper behind the veil. We are not their judge but leave that up to
the Lord.

Let us take delight in God's thoughts and words. His Word is
a treasure greater than all the gold and silver we could accumulate.
When we seek riches, we are reminded that the Word of God is more
valuable than precious gems. In our Bibles is all the self-help we will
ever need.

Step 87

• •

Forever, O Lord, Your word is settled in heaven.
Your faithfulness endures to all generations;
You established the earth, and it abides.
Unless Your law had been my delight,
I would then have perished in my affliction.
I will never forget Your precepts,
For by them You have given me life.
I am Yours, save me;
For I have sought Your precepts.
—Psalm 119:89–90, 92–94 (NKJV)

God's Word is accepted and honored in the heavens. His Word is also true throughout the earth even though some people are slow and rebellious to accept it. Whether it is believed or not, it doesn't change anything. It is still the gold standard for life.

It is because of God's Word, Jesus, that we are loved and saved. If we did not believe it, this earthly life would be all we have. We delight in the Word of God, and by it, we have the promise of eternal life. Because we believe in the Son of God, we belong to Him forever.

Through our life in Christ, we are becoming more and more like Him. The saved life is one of health, wholeness, and completeness. We are not perfect, but we are being made perfect. God doesn't make inferior people, and by His grace and the power of the Holy Spirit, we are precious in His sight.

So we live out each day in the hands of God being formed like a potter would and molded into the image of Jesus. We let Him have His way with us and conform us to His blueprint.

Step 88

● ●

Your word is a lamp to my feet And a light to my path.
Your testimonies I have taken as a heritage forever, For
they are the rejoicing of my heart. I have inclined my heart
to perform Your statutes Forever, to the very end.
—Psalm 119:105, 111–112 (NKJV)

When we don't know what steps to take, we are encouraged to trust the Lord and His Word, then we can see and know the way to go. Once we are moving, then we can trust the Word to show us which direction to take. So now we can make the necessary turns and corrections. God's Word enlightens our path so we are not confused or lost in the darkness.

The journey is easier when we know we are walking in the light. Jesus is our light and life. In Him, we are secure and fulfilling the call. Our choices can lead to derailment, but following Jesus leads to success and fulfillment.

When our lives are over and done on earth, let it be said about us that we were people of the Word. When someone had a question, we would give an answer based on and governed by the Word. We know that each decision we make must be in alignment with the Word, and that we are to have a history of right choices. The Word of God is a guardrail at dangerous curves and a bridge over unsettled waters.

Step 89

• •

Your testimonies are wonderful;
Therefore my soul keeps them.
The entrance of Your words gives light;
It gives understanding to the simple.
Direct my steps by Your word,
And let no iniquity have dominion over me.
Make Your face shine upon Your servant,
And teach me Your statutes.
—Psalm 119:129–130,133, 135 (NKJV)

It is wonderful when the Lord speaks directly to our heart or from the printed Word. We open ourselves to the Word of God and allow His light to illuminate us. We will hold tight to them and seek to understand His instruction to us. It is our desire to be lifted up and to abide by the Word.

We allow God to direct our steps and show us what course of action to take. It begins with realizing our own uncertainty and asking the Holy Spirit to answer us.

The Lord helps us to identify any sin that is blocking our understanding. It could be pride or impatience that is getting in the way of moving forward. We cast out any sin that is interfering with our obedience to God in the name of Jesus. Then we can let the light come into our soul and allow His face to shine upon us.

We are willing students who need the instruction of the Lord to carry on and fulfill the tasks that God has asked us to do. Praise God for His grace and mercy toward us.

Step 90

● ●

I rejoice at Your word
As one who finds great treasure.
Great peace have those who love Your law,
And nothing causes them to stumble.
Lord, I hope for Your salvation,
And I do Your commandments.
My soul keeps Your testimonies,
And I love them exceedingly.
I keep Your precepts and Your testimonies,
For all my ways are before You.
—Psalm 119:162, 165–168 (NKJV)

God's ways are righteousness, loving-kindness, salvation, truth, and judgment, and all these are our ways except for judgment that we leave to Him.

The treasure of God's Word is without measure. With it, we have new life, hope, and peace. Everything we need to live this life is contained in it.

The task before us is to dig out the truth of His Word. We know we are saved because Jesus loves us so much that He gave His life for us. We are righteous because we received it as a free gift from Jesus. Without God's truth, we go astray and become lost sheep without a shepherd.

We love the Word of God, and by keeping it, we do not stumble. It is life to our souls and revives us as we study it. When we speak His Word, we are the smartest people in the room. The Holy Spirit brings His commandments and precepts to our attention at just the right moment.

The ways of the world and our ways fall short when compared to God's ways. We praise God for the supernatural that exceeds all that we could hope for.

Step 91

• •

I will lift up my eyes to the hills—From whence comes my help?
My help comes from the Lord, Who made heaven and earth.
He will not allow your foot to be moved; He who keeps you will
not slumber. The Lord shall preserve you from all evil; He shall
preserve your soul. The Lord shall preserve your going out and
your coming in From this time forth, and even forevermore.
—Psalm 121:1–3 (NKJV)

Our help does not come from the hills or the earth or the heavens,
but it comes from the One who created it all. The Lord is full of
loving-kindness to us and is mighty to save. The Holy Spirit is our
counselor, our strength, our comforter, and our helper.

Our God (Holy Spirit) is always on duty looking out for us,
watching our every move, listening to every word, and bringing His
thoughts to our minds. He keeps track of us, wherever we may wander, gently nudging us along the right path. He is never too busy to
look out for us and keep us from error and danger.

The devil is out to derail our plans and to knock us off course.
But God is looking out for us. He knows our comings and goings
and is right there with us. He will not let out lives come to ruin or
allow us to spoil any opportunities to honor Him and bring glory to
His name.

The Lord is invested in us. We are His children. When the
storms come, He leads us to safety and spreads His wings to protect
us. In His care and companionship, there is security and joy, and
so today, He is looking into our faces and seeing if we won't crack a
smile. Our hearts are to join with His heart and complete this journey to heaven and beyond.

Step 92

Unless the Lord builds the house,
They labor in vain who build it;
Unless the Lord guards the city,
The watchman stays awake in vain.
Behold, children are a heritage from the Lord,
The fruit of the womb is a reward.
Like arrows in the hand of a warrior,
So are the children of one's youth.
Happy is the man who has his quiver full of them;
They shall not be ashamed,
But shall speak with their enemies in the gate.
—Psalm 127:1, 3–5 (NKJV)

When the Lord is over the home, the family has a higher probability of staying together and being prosperous. This is the place of basic training in allowing the Lord to rule over our lives. A home environment that relies solely on the things of the world takes a great risk.

What an awesome privilege and responsibility it is to raise children in the way they should go. Children are a gift from God and need to be treated as such. Parents who abide by the Word of God and the direction of the Holy Spirit are more likely to be rewarded in their efforts to equip their children.

As challenging and scary as it is to send children into the world, it is rewarding too. When we have taught our kids solid godly principles, we can be confident we have done our best. It's up to that child to take those Christian teachings with them and raise their offspring in the same way.

God knows it's not easy to bring up children, but He also wants to be a part of the process. God designed us to reproduce, to parent, and to build strong Christian families and homes.

Step 93

● ●

If You, Lord, should mark iniquities, O Lord, who could stand?
But there is forgiveness with You, That You may be feared. I
wait for the Lord, my soul waits, And in His word I do hope.
My soul waits for the Lord More than those who watch for the
morning—Yes, more than those who watch for the morning.
—Psalm 130:3–6 (NKJV)

How is it that God does not count our sins against us? God hates sin
and judged sin in the past, and He doesn't change. So how do sinners
like you and me escape His judgment? It is because Jesus has taken
all our sins past, present, and future. Not only were our sins placed
upon Him but also God's judgment. This was God's plan from the
beginning because He knew man's vulnerability to sin. The slate has
been wiped clean, and we have been forgiven because of God's love
for us.

So moving forward it is by the power of the Holy Spirit we are
able to overcome sin in our lives. In addition, we stand on the Word
of God which tells us the devil has been defeated. When he tempts
us to sin, we claim the name and the blood of Jesus as our Savior,
and he must flee. The devil's power over us is greatly diminished and
going away.

One day, we will leave this earth and the curse of sin. We put
our hope and trust in Jesus Christ and wait for the day when our
salvation will be complete.

Step 94

• •

> Let us go into His tabernacle; Let us worship at
> His footstool. Let Your priests be clothed with
> righteousness, And let Your saints shout for joy.
> —Psalm 132:7, 9 (NKJV)

> Behold, how good and how pleasant it is For
> brethren to dwell together in unity!
> —Ps 133:1 (NKJV)

> Behold, bless the Lord, All you servants of the Lord,
> Who by night stand in the house of the Lord! Lift up
> your hands in the sanctuary, And bless the Lord.
> —Psalm 134:1 (NKJV)

We can go into the throne room of heaven because the veil has been parted, and Jesus has invited us in to worship. It is there that we come to Jesus in humility and thanksgiving to worship at His feet. We have become the righteousness of the Lord, and our hearts shout for joy.

What satisfaction we feel when we worship with other believers in unity! Each life-giving church has its own unique style of worship. What unifies us is our honor and praise of Jesus as the head of our churches. We are to bless each church for the work they do and to encourage them.

Praise and worship can be formal or informal, strict, or relaxed but done in order. The important thing is to extol the name of Jesus and honor in the congregation. For the best participation and expression, the praise leader is led by the Holy Spirit. Spirit led praise and worship is genuine, honest, and from the heart. And don't be surprised if someone lifts their hands or claps or steps in the aisle to dance. It's all about glorifying the Lord in His sanctuary.

Step 95

• •

Praise the Lord, for the Lord is good;
Sing praises to His name, for it is pleasant.
For I know that the Lord is great,
And our Lord is above all gods.
Whatever the Lord pleases He does,
In heaven and in earth,
In the seas and in all deep places.
—Psalm 135:3, 5–6 (NKJV)

Our Lord is great, and we praise His holy name. Whatever pleases Him to do, He does it without hesitation. The Lord who made the heavens sees them in ways we cannot imagine. He acts alone and in ways He knows are best. Because He is timeless, He sees the beginning from the end and everything in between.

Our Lord is sovereign; He acts out of love and wisdom. He is the One and only true God; there are no other gods before Him. He is the ever present, all-knowing, timeless, and eternal God. He is three in one, one in three, Father, Son, and Holy Spirit. He is the God of grace and mercy we love, respect, and reverence.

When we pray, God answers our prayers but not always as we hoped for. As we pray according to His will, we are happy with the answer. But when we pray amiss, the answer can be no or not now. God always knows what is best for us, and He is looking out for us no matter what we pray. He wants to hear from us and speak to us through His Word and actions. We are being equipped to stand strong by the power of the Holy Spirit no matter what comes our way.

Step 96

I will praise You with my whole heart;
Before the gods I will sing praises to You.
I will worship toward Your holy temple,
And praise Your name
For Your lovingkindness and Your truth;
For You have magnified Your word above all Your name.
In the day when I cried out, You answered me,
And made me bold with strength in my soul.
Though the Lord is on high,
Yet He regards the lowly;
But the proud He knows from afar.
The Lord will perfect that which concerns me.
—Psalm 138:1–3, 6, 8a (NKJV)

The Lord looks out for the lowly and humble but ignores the proud. We must be vigilant in our lives to keep a good distance from pride. Pride, egotism, and selfishness are a nasty mix that keeps us from enjoying the loving kindness of the Lord.

We are encouraged to humbly come before the Lord into His throne room with praise and worship. We must remember that it is only by the grace of God and His mercy that we amount to anything. In His presence, we can ask what we will, and He will answer us. At His Word, we are made strong and can worship Him with boldness and confidence that we are His children and belong to the kingdom of God.

The good work that He has begun in us He is faithful to complete. We are beautiful pieces of pottery that the Lord is molding. We are masterpieces of art that the great artist is painting. We are sheep that were lost that the shepherd has found and brought back into the fold. Whatever the Lord desires of us, we are to give to Him in service and in love. He has not forsaken us, and His mercy endures forever.

Step 97

• •

O Lord, You have searched me and known me. You know my
sitting down and my rising up; You understand my thought
afar off. You comprehend my path and my lying down, And
are acquainted with all my ways. For there is not a word on my
tongue, But behold, O Lord, You know it altogether. You have
hedged me behind and before, And laid Your hand upon me. Such
knowledge is too wonderful for me; It is high, I cannot attain it.
—Psalm 139:1–6 (NKJV)

If we allow Him, the Lord will inspire our thinking, control our
tongue, influence our decisions, and guide our journey through life.
But if we ignore His presence, turn away from Him, and then we
reject a ready and powerful influence for good.

The Lord who created all life already knows everything about
us. He is aware of every thought we have, each decision we are about
to make, and steps we are going to take. His desire is to be a part of
every aspect of our lives. We are presumptuous, prideful, and foolish
to think we can do a better job of it and ignore His loving kindness.

His protection and care has brought us this far in life, so it is
time to give Him more of our lives. The all-knowing God sees our
lives as a moment in time. We want our lives to count for something more than just breathing and taking up space. He has us in His
hands, so let's not scurry away and try to hide.

The world presents challenges and obstacles too great for us to
overcome on our own. But to the Lord and His great power, they are
child's play to Him. It's silly to think we are up to the task on our
own when we can simply let go and let God have His way.

Step 98

● ●

> Where can I go from Your Spirit? Or where can I flee from Your presence? If I ascend into heaven, You are there; If I make my bed in hell, behold, You are there. If I take the wings of the morning, And dwell in the uttermost parts of the sea, Even there Your hand shall lead me, And Your right hand shall hold me.
> —Psalm 139:7–10 (NKJV)

Our God has this amazing quality of being everywhere at the same time. If we go on a trip, He is with us as we travel and when we reach our destination. God is with us when we lie down at night and when we wake in the morning. Every Christian around the world can experience the phenomena of God being with Him wherever He is. His guidance, wisdom, and protection are with us all the time.

The most important decision we can make in this life is to receive Jesus Christ as our Lord and Savior. We will make big decisions throughout our lives, but none have eternal consequences like choosing to follow Christ.

To reject Christ, His sacrifice for us and the gift of salvation has eternal consequences. That person will be constantly reminded of the really stupid choice he has made. When he wakes up at the judgment, he will realize that he could have had deliverance from the pit of hell and will regret it eternally.

However, for us, heaven is waiting, and Christ is calling us up to be with Him forever. Our lives are in His hands forever. We can only imagine how good heaven will be, but we know in our hearts that we don't want to miss it.

Step 99

●●●●●●●●●●●●●●●●●●●●●●●●●●●●●●●●●●

> For You formed my inward parts; You covered me in my
> mother's womb. I will praise You, for I am fearfully and
> wonderfully made; Marvelous are Your works, And that my
> soul knows very well. My frame was not hidden from You,
> When I was made in secret, And skillfully wrought in the
> lowest parts of the earth. Your eyes saw my substance, being yet
> unformed. And in Your book they all were written, The days
> fashioned for me, When as yet there were none of them.
> —Psalm 139:13–16 (NKJV)

How precious is the thought that God knew us as we were being
formed in the womb. He was involved in our formation, and that
we were skillfully put together. We are not accidents, and we are not
evolved from the apes.

On the sixth day of creation, God made man in His image. God
breathed life into His masterpiece, and life in the image of God has
been reproduced ever since. It is a relief to know that life and creation
didn't just occur by chance over millions of years.

Just looking at the mechanism of the human body assures us
that we are of a divine plan. If our eyes are open, we see the wonderful and amazing hand of God in the design of life. If we think that
we are too fat or too stupid, then we need to remember that we are
wonderfully made and part of God's marvelous works.

We are individually and uniquely put together, and no two
of us are the same. God lovingly and carefully made sure we came
forth according to His plan. Our lives are precious in the sight of our
Creator God.

Step 100

• •

How precious also are Your thoughts to me, O God!
How great is the sum of them! If I should count them,
they would be more in number than the sand;
When I awake, I am still with You.
Search me, O God, and know my heart;
Try me, and know my anxieties;
And see if there is any wicked way in me,
And lead me in the way everlasting.
—Psalm 139:17–18, 23–24 (NKJV)

What kind of thoughts does God have toward us? They are good, thoughts of love and concern, not of anger or evil. God is thinking of our safety and protecting us from the hazards of this world. He wants to make sure we are growing in wisdom and faith.

His desire is to use us in some small way to move His kingdom forward. God is looking for ways to bless us on our journey. He wants to take us out of selfishness and rebellion to a place of mutual love. He covets our worship, desires an intimacy with us, and to answer our prayers. He would like an ongoing dialog with us and a partnership as we go through these days together. These are only some of the precious thoughts God has for us.

Our response is to be open and cooperative to Him. We are to be humble enough to let God examine our hearts for any evil thought that might be holding us back. We have to be willing to trust Him and let Him remove any fear we have in the present and for tomorrow. If there is sin or darkness in the corners of our hearts, we have to let God remove it from us. The Holy Spirit desires to be our helper and our guide. Are we willing to partner with Him?

Step 101

● ●

I remember the days of old; I meditate on all Your works; I muse
on the work of Your hands. I spread out my hands to You;
My soul longs for You like a thirsty land.
Cause me to hear Your lovingkindness in the morning,
For in You do I trust;
Cause me to know the way in which I should walk,
For I lift up my soul to You.
Teach me to do Your will,
For You are my God;
Your Spirit is good.
Lead me in the land of uprightness.
—Psalm 143:5–6, 8, 10 (NKJV)

We remember our younger days when we did not follow You and
thought the things of God were foolish. We were caught up in intel-
lectualism and secular humanism until we saw the folly of our ways.
You showed us the error of our ways and led us back to the truth.
Now we meditate on all Your works and marvel at the complexity of
the smallest flower.

Our souls hunger and thirst after You to be delivered from sin
and to walk in righteousness. Good intentions are commendable,
but the leading and power of the Holy Spirit is required to stay on
the right path. Cause us to hear You and to walk in Your loving kindness. We can only trust in the God of creation who calls us to come
near to Him.

Teach us how to live each day with purpose and productively.
Let our last days have meaning and reason to be your disciples. Give
us a taste of Your wisdom that we might focus on what action you
want for our lives. May our thoughts be turned to You and away
from selfishness and self-centered behavior that is futile and wasteful
of our time.

Step 102

•••••••••••••••••••••••••••••••

Lord, what is man, that You take knowledge of him? Or the son
of man, that You are mindful of him? Man is like a breath;
His days are like a passing shadow.
That our sons may be as plants grown up in their youth;
That our daughters may be as pillars,
Sculptured in palace style;
That our barns may be full,
Supplying all kinds of produce;
That our sheep may bring forth thousands
And ten thousands in our fields;
Happy are the people who are in such a state;
Happy are the people whose God is the Lord!
—Psalm 144:3–4, 12–13, 15 (NKJV)

It's not who we are that is important, but who God is. He knows us
inside and out for our brief moment on earth. God has been mindful of us before we were born, and He will continue to think of us
throughout eternity. Not only does He care for us but our family as
well. Our prayers for our sons and daughters God answers so that
they will be strong and followers of Jesus Christ.

God's desire is for us to prosper in whatever we put our hands
and our minds to. He provides just enough things that all of our
needs are taken care of. He will not let His people go hungry and
sees to it that we are clothed and sheltered. We do not expect great
monetary wealth, but we realize that we are rich beyond measure
compared to the rest of the world.

Finally, God released a supernatural joy in us that is the envy of
those around us. This joy has the power to put our minds at rest and
our souls at peace. It's because we have a heavenly Father who loves
us and fills us with hope unending.

Step 103

• •

I will extol You, my God, O King; And I will bless Your name forever and ever. Every day I will bless You, And I will praise Your name forever and ever. Great is the Lord, and greatly to be praised; And His greatness is unsearchable. One generation shall praise Your works to another, And shall declare Your mighty acts. I will meditate on the glorious splendor of Your majesty, And on Your wondrous works. Men shall speak of the might of Your awesome acts, And I will declare Your greatness. They shall utter the memory of Your great goodness, And shall sing of Your righteousness.
—Psalm 145:1–7 (NKJV)

Every day, we will lift up the name of the Father and the Son in praise and worship forever. We will praise God for as long as we live and are able because He is great. We only know a little of His greatness, but we will express what we know from His Word and our experience. We will pass on to the next generation what we have learned, and they will add their insight to it. The hand of God is great and mighty and at work in each generation.

When we meditate on God's works, we get to know Him better. His majesty, splendor, and wondrous works are too great for us to comprehend. We can only declare to others what the Holy Spirit has shown us and pass it on. It is a pleasure and an honor to speak of how good God has been to us. No one can dispute our testimony of the greatness of God. We have seen it and experienced His mighty power. We will not keep silent and will continue to marvel and wonder about our gracious and merciful God.

Step 104

•••••••••••••••••••••••••••••••••

The Lord is gracious and full of compassion, Slow to anger and great in mercy. The Lord is good to all, And His tender mercies are over all His works. All Your works shall praise You, O Lord, And Your saints shall bless You. They shall speak of the glory of Your kingdom, And talk of Your power, To make known to the sons of men His mighty acts, And the glorious majesty of His kingdom. Your kingdom is an everlasting kingdom, And Your dominion endures throughout all generations. The Lord upholds all who fall, And raises up all who are bowed down. The eyes of all look expectantly to You, And You give them their food in due season. You open Your hand And satisfy the desire of every living thing.
—Psalm 145:8–16 (NKJV)

The Lord is full of grace and mercy. He is compassionate, kind, and good. Even though we fall short, God is merciful and slow to anger toward us. He understands what we are going through and allows negative situations to be our teacher. He is patient with us in our weaknesses and picks us up when we stumble.

We are a work in progress. Jesus as a man was tempted in all ways and yet did not sin. He sets the bar higher and knows we cannot pass the test without the power of the Holy Spirit. The Holy Spirit has come as another One like Jesus to be our strength in time of need. This is the way God upholds us and raises us up.

We look to Him with hope and expectation that every need will be met. What a great and caring God we serve. We will praise Him and talk of His power and majesty. His kingdom is forever, and He rules throughout all generations.

Step 105

• •

The Lord is righteous in all His ways, Gracious in all His works. The Lord is near to all who call upon Him, To all who call upon Him in truth. He will fulfill the desire of those who fear Him; He also will hear their cry and save them. The Lord preserves all who love Him, But all the wicked He will destroy. My mouth shall speak the praise of the Lord, And all flesh shall bless His holy name Forever and ever.
—Psalm 145:17–21 (NKJV)

Righteousness belongs to the Lord, and we became righteous when we accepted Jesus as our Lord and Savior. The Lord is gracious in all of His ways, and we receive love, kindness, and goodness from Him. As Christians, the Lord is near to us. He has become intimate with us and desires a personal relationship.

We are to cry out to Him in our need, and He will hear us and fulfill our desire. The truth is He will come near to us as we call upon His name. Praises to our God will be constantly on our lips. In return, He blesses us constantly forever and ever.

The Lord watches out for His people because of His love for them. He is the best Father anyone could ever hope for. He instructs us through the Word, who is His Son, Jesus Christ. The Holy Spirit who points us to Jesus, and the gospel fills us with wisdom and truth.

We are equipped to do all that God asks of us and what to say in stressful situations. The Spirit reminds us of the plan the Father has for us and keeps us on the right path.

Step 106

• •

Praise the Lord!
Praise the Lord, O my soul!
While I live I will praise the Lord;
I will sing praises to my God while I have my being.
Do not put your trust in princes,
Nor in a son of man, in whom there is no help.
Happy is he who has the God of Jacob for his help,
Whose hope is in the Lord his God,
The Lord shall reign forever—
Your God, O Zion, to all generations.
Praise the Lord!
—Psalm 146:1–3,5 10 (NKJV)

We put our hope and trust in the Lord. It is good to have a job and a career, but they are fleeting and temporary. Factories move away and businesses close; we know because we have seen the employment situation change and look different from only a few years ago. We will work hard and respect our bosses, but we know the business environment is in transition.

Government leadership comes and goes with each election cycle. A pet program popular with one political party may disappear with the new incoming officials. So we can't get too comfortable with the party currently in control because they may be gone at the next election cycle.

However, our God and His government never changes. He is the same yesterday, today, and forever. The gospel business is always available and prospering. So we put our trust in a truthful, all-powerful, and eternal God. And as an extra bonus, that is where we find true happiness. Glory and honor to our God today!

Step 107

He heals the brokenhearted
and binds up their wounds.
He counts the number of the stars;
He calls them all by name.
Great is our Lord, and mighty in power;
His understanding is infinite.
He does not delight in the strength of the horse;
He takes no pleasure in the legs of a man.
The Lord takes pleasure in those who fear Him,
In those who hope in His mercy.
For He has strengthened the bars of your gates;
He has blessed your children within you.
He makes peace in your borders,
and fills you with the finest wheat.
—Psalm 147:3–5, 10–11, 13–14 (NKJV)

The Lord is an expert at healing the brokenhearted. The world with its good intentions fails to lift those that feel defeated and discouraged. The path to success is littered with broken dreams, sickness, and hopelessness. But God lifts us up, dusts us off, binds our wounds, and put us on a path to salvation and victory.

Those who reject the Lord's help are depending on their own strength. What a lonely, frustrating, and difficult way to go. God puts a choice before us to live life without Him or to humble ourselves before Him and accept his help.

God desires to bless us with the best. He takes pleasure in those that trust Him and put their hope in the Creator of all life. He wants to fill our lives with good things and prosper us in all we put our hands to. The Holy Spirit will provide the wisdom, strength, and resources we need. God desires to surround us with His loving-kindness and peace. As we open ourselves to Him, He comes in and takes up residence with us.

Step 108

● ●

> Praise the Lord! Praise God in His sanctuary; Praise Him
> in His mighty firmament! Praise Him for His mighty acts;
> Praise Him according to His excellent greatness! Praise Him
> with the sound of the trumpet; Praise Him with the lute
> and harp! Praise Him with the timbrel and dance; Praise
> Him with stringed instruments and flutes! Praise Him
> with loud cymbals; Praise Him with clashing cymbals! Let
> everything that has breath praise the Lord. Praise the Lord!
> —Psalm 150 (NKJV)

All living things have been called upon to praise the Lord. Trees wave their branches, and flowers raise their heads to heaven. Even the earth and its seas praise their Creator.

So we the life-giving church raise our voices in praise to the Lord. Let our sanctuaries erupt in song and dance. For those who don't know the Lord will see and hear our praises to the life-giving Lord.

Let's join the symphony of praise that is sounding through-out the universe. We are thankful for our God who has opened the throne room to His people. We are thankful for a release of the Holy Spirit who comforts, strengthens, and gives us wisdom. We are especially thankful for Jesus who came to dwell with mankind, showed us how to live, and died on a cross so that we might live. How can we not be stirred to praise and worship the one true God who we will spend eternity with? Let everything that has breath praise the Lord. Praise the Lord!

Step 109

●●●●●●●●●●●●●●●●●●●●●●●●●●●●●●●●

A wise man will hear and increase learning, and a
man of understanding will attain wise counsel.
—Proverbs 1:5 (NKJV)

It seems the more we know we realize, there is so much more to take
in. We have barely scratched the surface. The brain has an amazing
capacity to absorb and retain knowledge. But when is it enough? As
long as we are able, we are to continue to learn and to use our ears
to hear. To be wise is to continually sort through the storehouse of
knowledge we have. We can update the old thinking with the new
ways of seeing things. Open eyes and open ears take in new ideas.
Wisdom allows us to sort through our knowledge bank and toss out
the useless and keep the practical. The Holy Spirit is a great teacher
and source of wisdom.

"The fear of the Lord is the beginning of knowledge,
But fools despise wisdom and instruction"
—Proverbs 1:7 (NKJV)

The Lord is the ultimate source of wisdom. To reverence, the
Lord is to open the door to the greatest storehouse of knowledge.
The Creator of the universe and all life is who we want to be in contact with through the Holy Spirit. Studying His Word reveals His
wisdom to us. The Holy Spirit will reveal the deeper things of God to
us as we seek to know more. To think we don't need God's wisdom or
to believe we can learn all we need to know on our own is foolishness.
Let's turn to God, ask Him for His help, and open ourselves to Him.

Step 110

●●●●●●●●●●●●●●●●●●●●●●●●●●●●●●●●●●

My son, if you receive my words, and treasure my commands
within you, So that you incline your ear to wisdom, And apply
your heart to understanding; Yes, if you cry out for discernment,
And lift up your voice for understanding, if you seek her as
silver, and search for her as for hidden treasures; Then you will
understand the fear of the Lord, and find the knowledge of God.
—Proverbs 2:1–5 (NKJV)

The wisdom of the Lord does not come without some effort. Gold
and silver do not lay on the ground, instead it is hidden underground.
A successful miner must know where to dig and then create a tunnel
underground. Sometimes the miner must dig for a long time before
the treasure is discovered.

This is also true for the student of the Word seeking to know
God's wisdom. A casual reading of the scriptures might reveal a nugget of truth, but it's only the start to finding the deeper things of
God. The Holy Spirit is available to guide us to the treasure of God's
wisdom we need to meet the challenges of life.

The miner is highly motivated to discover the treasure after
finding a hint of silver or gold. We must desire strongly the wisdom
of God with open ears and an eager heart. We must understand how
to reverence our God and find His knowledge.

We know that "fool's gold" has no value and is discarded as
worthless. A wrong interpretation and application of God's Word is a
similar situation. We cry out to God to give us discernment of truth
and error. It is in partnership with the Holy Spirit that we find the
valuable treasures of God's wisdom.

Step 111

● ●

For the Lord gives wisdom; From His mouth come knowledge
and understanding; He stores up sound wisdom for the upright;
He is a shield to those who walk uprightly; He guards the paths
of justice, and preserves the way of His saints. Then you will
understand righteousness and justice, equity and every good path.
—Proverbs 2:6–9 (NKJV)

There is no wisdom on earth to compare with what comes from God's knowledge and understanding. There is no question He can't answer, nor request He will not consider. His reply may not be what we imagined or hoped for. The ways of the God are higher and deeper than those of mankind. His truth, goodness, righteousness, and fairness are the hallmarks of His kingdom. He has invited us into His kingdom and shown us how to enter in.

The Holy Spirit is our guide to the pathways of God. By acknowledging and accepting the sacrifice of Jesus Christ, we are worthy to walk in the pathways of righteousness and to be called children of God.

By following God's way, we are safe and secure in His grace and compassion. As we study the things of God, we grow in His wisdom and truth. Although we can't see God, we sense His presence and encouragement to keep going and to reach higher than we have before. As we listen for His voice in the quiet times and seek Him through His Word, we grow up and mature.

Step 112

··

When wisdom enters your heart, and knowledge is
pleasant to your soul, Discretion will preserve you;
Understanding will keep you,
So you may walk in the way of goodness,
and keep to the paths of righteousness.
For the upright will dwell in the land,
and the blameless will remain in it.
—Proverbs 2:10–11, 20–21 (NKJV)

To know God's Word is to study the scriptures and allow them to
sink into our hearts. Having accepted them as truth, we proceed to
understand what they mean and how they could be applied to our
lives. Every situation has a right or wrong choice and can have a good
or bad outcome. God's wisdom helps us to make the best choice. To
walk in God's ways brings peace and comfort to our minds, will, and
emotions. The Holy Spirit is our guide to use what we know and
what we don't know to send us in the right direction.

Using God's wisdom releases His blessings and goodness into
our lives. Knowing God's Word fills a reservoir in our hearts to draw
upon. Accumulated knowledge carries us through the most difficult
and trying times. When we get to heaven, imagine the joy we will
experience as more of God's wisdom is added to the basic ingredients
we gathered on earth. It is more than the human mind can fathom!

Step 113

• •

My son, do not forget my law, but let your heart keep my
commands; for length of days and long life and peace they will
add to you. Let not mercy and truth forsake you; bind them
around your neck, write them on the tablet of your heart, and
so find favor and high esteem in the sight of God and man.
—Proverbs 3:1–4 (NKJV)

It is our desire to keep the Word of God in our hearts and to remember the key passages. By doing so, we have the opportunity to live a full twenty-four-hour day that honors the Lord. As much as possible, we want these days to add up to a complete and satisfied life. Let us season our lives with the peace of God that is beyond understanding.

We can live these kinds of days knowing that God is not judging us because all our sins have been put on Jesus Christ our Lord. As a kind and loving Father, He leads us into all truth. There is worldly truth and godly truth which do not always agree. Let us be led by the latter.

When the Word of God is solidly established in our hearts, we experience favor with mankind. But more importantly, we are in an intimate relationship with our Father God. He sees us as worthy of His promises and blessings.

Step 114

● ●

> Trust in the Lord with all your heart, and lean
> not on your own understanding; In all your ways
> acknowledge Him, and He shall direct your paths.
> —Proverbs 3:5–6 (NKJV)

In all things and situations, we will trust the Lord. We will depend on Him for our finances, our health, our thoughts, and our choices. No matter how bad things might get, we will trust the Lord for the best outcome.

Our own understanding of the situation will take second place to the Lord's wisdom. We may think we have the right answer, but we will check with the Lord first. The old egotistical self may appear to know what direction to go but will need to yield to a higher power.

We will seek the Lord in the simplest to the most complex problem. Our relationship to the Lord can be depended on to lead us in the right direction. We live each moment in intimacy with our Lord and Savior.

As we look back on our lives, we see the hand of the Lord at work. We might think that we did it all on our own, but the Lord's presence was key to our success. When we ignore the Lord's leading, we open ourselves up for a teaching moment.

Step 115

Do not be wise in your own eyes; Fear the Lord and depart
from evil. It will be health to your flesh, and strength to your
bones. Honor the Lord with your possessions, and with the
first fruits of all your increase; So your barns will be filled
with plenty, and your vats will overflow with new wine.
—Proverbs 3:7–10 (NKJV)

To be wise in your own eyes is to be in pride and lacking in humility. We are to be wise in the eyes of the Lord and drawing upon His wisdom. Ignoring the Lord or even turning from Him opens us up to sin and all manner of evil from the devil.

The enemy uses all sorts of temptation to draw us away from the Lord. Sin results in regret, disappointment, loss, darkness, damage, and entrapment that is hard to escape. At its worst, it can lead to poverty, sickness, disease, and even death. But reverence for the Lord will release health and strength into our souls and bodies.

The Lord is the source of all our prosperity. The tithe is a tenth of all we have received from Him. We are to give a portion of all He has given us for use in His kingdom. Our gifts and talents are to be presented to the honor and glory of the Lord.

An amazing kingdom principle is that as we give, He gives back to us. A faithful giver will experience a significant return and blessings from the Lord. Pride and stinginess will keep us locked up and struggling to make ends meet.

Step 116

• •

My son, do not despise the chastening of the Lord,
nor detest His correction; for whom the Lord loves He
corrects, just as a father the son in whom he delights.
—Proverbs 3:11–12 (NKJV)

If we are honest, we will admit we make a ton of mistakes in this Christian life. Every day there is a thought, spoken word, wrong emotion, or action that we wish we could take back. But it's too late and already out there, and the Lord has witnessed it because He is all-knowing.

Our first reaction is something like shame, regret, or remorse that it has happened. How could we let that slip up or sin occur? Well, we are not perfect but being perfected. We are a work in progress, and it won't be complete until we get to heaven.

However, it's good to know that Jesus has already taken our sins. We are washed clean and purified in His blood. If we confess our wrongdoings, He is faithful and just to forgive us. Each day, we are getting a little closer to that total perfection.

As children, none of us enjoyed being corrected by our parents. And growing up, there was correction that came from teachers, bosses, law enforcement, and well-meaning loved ones and family. Even lawyers and judges can bring correction. Doctors and nurses will speak into our lives.

Since the Lord knows of our shortcomings, He is available to bring correction. God is a loving Father to us who gently nudges us back on the correct path when we stray. The mistakes we make can be turned into growth and maturity. There is a place we can get to in this life where we can see that the Lord's correction was good and necessary to keep us moving forward according to His plan.

Step 117

● ●

Happy is the man who finds wisdom, and the man who gains
understanding; For her proceeds are better than the profits of
silver, and her gain than fine gold. She is more precious than
rubies, and all the things you may desire cannot compare
with her. Length of days is in her right hand, in her left
hand riches and honor. Her ways are ways of pleasantness,
and all her paths are peace. She is a tree of life to those
who take hold of her, and happy are all who retain her.
—Proverbs 3:13–18 (NKJV)

Divine wisdom is a contributor to happiness. To tap into God's wisdom brings a smile to our faces because we know we have connected with the supernatural. How pleasing it is to source genuine truth over the superficial, ever changing, and the temporary.

With the Creator's wisdom, creativity is released and realized. That is so valuable in our lives and worth opening up to. This is a place of richer life and peace. Happiness and contentment are the results of tapping into this wisdom.

The secret is to build upon life's knowledge and experience by adding divine wisdom. That puts us on a golden path into a rich life of heaven on earth. Isn't that life a reward worth seeking? Let's keep pressing in for the more that God has for us.

Step 118

My son, let them not depart from your eyes—Keep sound wisdom and discretion; So they will be life to your soul and grace to your neck. Then you will walk safely in your way, and your foot will not stumble. When you lie down, you will not be afraid; Yes, you will lie down and your sleep will be sweet. Do not be afraid of sudden terror, Nor of trouble from the wicked when it comes; For the Lord will be your confidence, and will keep your foot from being caught.
—Proverbs 3:21–26 (NKJV)

Out hiking on an icy snow-packed trail, there are multiple opportunities to slip and fall. However, with crampons attached to our boots, we are safe and secure. On the path of life, we may stumble, but the Lord will keep us from falling.

As we lie down to sleep for the night, our brains continue to process all that happened through the day and in the past. The enemy loves to sneak in and disrupt our sleep with bad dreams and nightmares. We say a prayer before going to sleep that the Lord will calm our fears and release us into a sweet sleep.

No matter where we live, we are subject to sudden natural terrors. It might be an earthquake or a tornado or a fire or maybe a flood to name a few. The Lord is our refuge and a strong tower against these disasters.

The enemy is out to disrupt our lives by coming around as a roaring lion. We must call on the name of Jesus so that the enemy and his demons flee. When we partner with the Holy Spirit, He keeps us safe and secure by guiding us on the right path.

Step 119

• •

> Do not withhold good from those to whom it is due, when
> it is in the power of your hand to do so. Do not say to your
> neighbor, "Go, and come back, and tomorrow I will give it,"
> When you have it with you. Do not devise evil against your
> neighbor, for he dwells by you for safety's sake. Do not strive
> with a man without cause, if he has done you no harm.
> —Proverbs 3:27–30 (NKJV)

We have opportunities to be generous to those around us if we are
alert and paying attention. Extra clothing that is no longer being
worn and doesn't fit anymore can be given to a clothes cottage. Extra
food in the cupboard can benefit someone at the local food give-
away. Most churches partner with charitable organizations to help
the needy. We often have more surplus than we realize that could
benefit someone else.

Some gifts are simple like a smile or a kind word. What a joy it
is to have neighbors that feel the same way. It is a blessing to live next
to someone you can trust and appreciate. We are instructed to love
our neighbors as ourselves. Let us live in peace with as many people
as possible.

Step 120

• •

Do not envy the oppressor, and choose none of his ways; For
the perverse person is an abomination to the Lord, but His
secret counsel is with the upright. The curse of the Lord is on
the house of the wicked, but He blesses the home of the just.
Surely He scorns the scornful, but gives grace to the humble. The
wise shall inherit glory, but shame shall be the legacy of fools.
—Proverbs 3:31–35 (NKJV)

We will not give in to the temptations of the enemy. Just as Jesus
resisted the enemy, we will stand on the Word and the promises of
God. The secret counsel of the Lord is what we seek and listen for.
Through prayer, intimacy, and fellowship with the Lord, we will hear
and follow His advice.

The Lord has blessed us with salvation and a redeemed life. He
has taken our sins to the cross, and we are washed clean in His blood.
We are sanctified and consecrated unto the Lord as one of His saints.

And yet we will not grow prideful but will remain humble and
walk in His grace toward us. We revel in His glory and always antici-
pate His return. As children of the Highest, we have a family of God
inheritance that cannot be stolen from us.

Step 121

● ●

Get wisdom! Get understanding! Do not forget, nor turn away from the words of my mouth. Do not forsake her, and she will preserve you; Love her, and she will keep you. Wisdom is the principal thing; Therefore get wisdom. And in all your getting, get understanding.
—Proverbs 4:5–7 (NKJV)

When we were young, there were various sources of learning available to us. Parents, schoolteachers, books, friends, bosses, and life experiences instructed us in how to live this life. The important thing was to be open to good teaching. Rebellion and egotism were enemies of our education. It was tempting to believe we knew better and close ourselves off to good instruction.

As we grew and matured, we realized that there was a greater source of knowledge and understanding. God's Word and His revelation were superior to anything we had learned before. Now we could enter in to everything we would need to live at the highest level.

Now that we have delved into God's Word, we have become equipped to handle whatever comes our way. When we opened the Bible and began to read, we were introduced to the deeper things of God and the real purpose of life.

God wants us to take His wisdom and apply it to all we have learned along the way. We can have a head full of facts and figures, but without wisdom, we are ill-equipped. God's wisdom helps us to be most effective and productive in this life.

Step 122

● ●

Exalt her, and she will promote you; she will bring you honor, when you embrace her. She will place on your head an ornament of grace; a crown of glory she will deliver to you." Hear, my son, and receive my sayings, and the years of your life will be many. I have taught you in the way of wisdom; I have led you in right paths. When you walk, your steps will not be hindered, and when you run, you will not stumble. Take firm hold of instruction, do not let go. Keep her, for she is your life.
—Proverbs 4:8-13 (NKJV)

Because we walk in God's wisdom, we wear the ornament of His grace (loving-kindness and goodness). A crown of glory is awaiting us who are faithful. Honor and blessings are presented to us. We will be blessed with as many days and years as it takes to perfect us.

Our lives are to be filled with God's wisdom and instruction. Only then we will walk in the paths of righteousness that are laid out for us and fulfill His plan for us. We will take a firm hold on these instructions from the Lord and not let them go.

In the process, the enemy will not hinder our steps and our mission, and destiny will be completed. When we are handed the baton, we will run the race and not stumble. We will keep a firm hold on this secret to a fulfilled life.

Step 123

● ●

But the path of the just is like the shining sun, that
shines ever brighter unto the perfect day.
My son, give attention to my words;
incline your ear to my sayings.
Do not let them depart from your eyes;
Keep them in the midst of your heart;
for they are life to those who find them,
and health to all their flesh.
—Proverbs 4:18, 20–22 (NKJV)

The Word of the Lord makes our path shine brighter against the darkness. It frustrates the enemy when we claim the Lord's Word whenever we are lost, afraid, confused, weak, angry, or sick. There is power in the Word as we quote it in a difficult situation. The Word is truth and can be used to change something that is wrong.

Sickness is not from God; there is no sickness or disease in heaven. We become ill because we live in a fallen world. But since we are members of the family of God and children of His kingdom, we claim a higher power. So sickness and disease have to yield to the spoken Word of God.

We all get sick at times and do not enjoy it. We are to use doctors, medicine, and rest to recover from illness. However, we have a secret weapon against sickness. It is the Word of God. When we sense symptoms coming on or our bodies under attack, we are to fight back with the Word of God.

We are to keep the Word in our midst, reading it, hearing it, and speaking it. It is powerful and health to our bodies. The more we use it against sickness, the healthier we become until we go to heaven and are completely healed.

Step 124

• •

> Keep your heart with all diligence, for out of it spring the
> issues of life. Put away from you a deceitful mouth, and put
> perverse lips far from you. Let your eyes look straight ahead,
> and your eyelids look right before you. Ponder the path of
> your feet, and let all your ways be established. Do not turn
> to the right or the left; Remove your foot from evil.
> —Proverbs 4:23–27 (NKJV)

The physical heart is an important pump for blood circulation in our physical life. It is enclosed in a sac and protected by bones and muscle. Just so is our spiritual heart the center of our spiritual well-being. We must protect and guard it against any penetration of darkness.

We must take captive all our thoughts for the glory of God. What we think can turn into words that proceed from our mouths. If we are not careful, negative thoughts and words and actions can contaminate our hearts.

What we look upon with our eyes can influence the thoughts of our hearts. There are good and bad things to see. We must guard our eye-gates into our hearts. Our visual and audio senses are positive or negative entryways into ourselves.

We are faced with choices every day that can be good or bad influences. We are to be thoughtful and careful considering our alternatives. God has laid out a path for us to take and has asked us to follow His way. The challenge is to make the right choice everyday under the guidance of the Holy Spirit.

Step 125

Does not wisdom cry out, and understanding lift up her voice?
She takes her stand on the top of the high hill, beside the way,
where the paths meet. She cries out by the gates, at the entry of
the city, at the entrance of the doors: "To you, O men, I call, and
my voice is to the sons of men. O you simple ones, understand
prudence, and you fools, be of an understanding heart.
—Proverbs 8:1–5 (NKJV)

God's wisdom is accessible to us and available to draw upon. It may
seem shrouded in secrecy, but it's not. It's as close as opening up our
Bible. It can be found by being still before the Lord. The Lord is
open to answering our questions and helping us solve problems.

God's wisdom is hidden from those who would mock Him or
doubt His presence. For unbelievers, it is the sound of silence and
unavailable. God will not hinder us from seeking other sources of
understanding or take away our free choice.

The Lord is looking for a humble heart that is open to Him and
who is tired of trying to figure it all out on his own. There comes
a point where we look to our own efforts and find them futile. We
must hunger and thirst after supernatural truth that exists in spite
of what is going on around us. Let's open our ears and hear from
heaven.

Step 126

• •

"The Lord possessed me at the beginning of His way, Before
His works of old. I have been established from everlasting, From
the beginning, before there was ever an earth. When there were
no depths I was brought forth, When there were no fountains
abounding with water. Before the mountains were settled, Before
the hills, I was brought forth; While as yet He had not made the
earth or the fields, Or the primal dust of the world. When He
prepared the heavens, I was there, When He drew a circle on the
face of the deep, When He established the clouds above, When
He strengthened the fountains of the deep, When He assigned
to the sea its limit, So that the waters would not transgress His
command, When He marked out the foundations of the earth,
Then I was beside Him as a master craftsman; And I was daily
His delight, Rejoicing always before Him, Rejoicing in His
inhabited world, And my delight was with the sons of men.
—Proverbs 8:22–31 (NKJV)

The wisdom of God is ancient, as old as God Himself, who is timeless. Creativity and imagination and excellence have existed with
God since the beginning. Wisdom is not a new thing; it has always
been with God. That same wisdom is stored in heaven for you and
me. He makes it available to us for whatever needs be. There is power
and strength in that wisdom. There is delight and joy for us to draw
upon. There are no limits to God's wisdom.

Step 127

• •

"Now therefore, listen to me, my children, for blessed are those who keep my ways. Hear instruction and be wise, and do not disdain it. Blessed is the man who listens to me, watching daily at my gates, waiting at the posts of my doors. For whoever finds me finds life, and obtains favor from the Lord.
—Proverbs 8:32–35 (NKJV)

We are to be constantly on alert for the next move of God in our lives or in the circumstances that surround us. Keeping our hearts attuned and listening for that still small voice from the Lord. We are to keep our eyes open and watching for a sign from Him. His timing is not our timing, so watching and waiting is what we do.

We are to keep ourselves pure and stay connected to the Holy Spirit. If we are closed to Him or into some sort of sin, we will miss Him. We are to be ready to be used of God in whatever way He may chose. His ways are not our ways, so we need a discerning spirit to detect His instructions.

It is a blessing from the Lord to be used mightily by Him. He uses people to accomplish His purposes here on earth. So we may not be the first choice by God, but we might be the only willing vessel at the time. Our voice may not be the most articulate or our appearance the most appealing, but we are to be ready anyway. To be used by God is to find favor and to be blessed by Him.

Step 128

● ●

Wisdom has built her house, she has hewn out her seven pillars;
She has slaughtered her meat, She has mixed her wine, She has
also furnished her table. She has sent out her maidens, She cries
out from the highest places of the city, "Whoever is simple, let
him turn in here!" As for him who lacks understanding, she says to
him, "Come, eat of my bread and drink of the wine I have mixed.
Forsake foolishness and live, and go in the way of understanding.
—Proverbs 9:1–6 (NKJV)

The provisions of wisdom are more than enough to satisfy us. To
come to the table of wisdom is to come to a sumptuous banquet.
From the simplest decision to the most complex problem, wisdom
provides the answer.

To live without God's wisdom is foolishness and futility. We
humble ourselves before the Lord and admit we don't know which
direction to go without Him. We can depend on the Holy Spirit to
show us the way and to clear away the fog.

Wisdom is solid and sturdy, a good place to live. To admit we
don't have all the answers and the ones we do have aren't too strong
is the starting place. It is in that place that the light of God's wisdom
shines and indicates the way.

We hunger and thirst after You Lord. Intimacy with You is our
strongest desire. You are the strong tower that we run to and feel safe
and satisfied in Your presence.

Step 129

● ●

Give instruction to a wise man, and he will be still wiser;
teach a just man, and he will increase in learning. "The fear
of the Lord is the beginning of wisdom, and the knowledge
of the Holy One is understanding. For by me your days will
be multiplied, and years of life will be added to you.
—Proverbs 9:9–11 (NKJV)

To be wise is to realize how little we know and to hunger after more.
To taste good food leads to more bites and a full meal. Wisdom
sounds good and looks good so that the heart desires all it can get.
Who is it that feels he knows enough and wants to stop learning?

The task before us is to learn as much about Jesus Christ, the
Holy One. Let's learn all we can about His ministry and purpose for
coming to earth as a man. The way He entered into human life and
the way He left it is important. God's timing is perfect so the coming
of Jesus two thousand years ago was significant. The fact that He
was perfect, was tempted, and did not sin cannot go unnoticed. He
crammed the wisdom of God into three and a half years of teaching.
He was the greatest teacher who ever taught on earth. He fulfilled
hundreds of Old Testament prophecies. He is the Messiah and sits at
the right hand of the Father interceding for us. At just the right time,
He will return again in glory and splendor.

The challenge before us is to learn as much about Jesus Christ
as we can. By doing so, we become more like Him and develop an
intimate relationship with Him. He modeled the Christian life and
showed us how to live it. When we have learned all, we can and are
unable to learn more, then we will graduate to heaven and eternity to
complete our education.

Step 130

● ●

The proverbs of Solomon: A wise son makes a glad father, But a foolish son is the grief of his mother. Treasures of wickedness profit nothing, But righteousness delivers from death. The Lord will not allow the righteous soul to famish, But He casts away the desire of the wicked. He who has a slack hand becomes poor, But the hand of the diligent makes rich. 5 He who gathers in summer is a wise son; He who sleeps in harvest is a son who causes shame. Blessings are on the head of the righteous, But violence covers the mouth of the wicked. The memory of the righteous is blessed, But the name of the wicked will rot.
—Proverbs 10:1–7 (NKJV)

We know that we could have done more to make our parents proud of us. Alas, that opportunity quickly passes. However, we are the righteousness of God, the Father, and children of His kingdom. Now chances abound to serve God, our heavenly Father.

He has blessed us mightily, and we look to bless Him back in our daily lives. We can never match or exceed all He has done for us. But let us be about the Lord's work putting our hand to the plow to reap a harvest from the field and bear fruit in His orchard.

We are to set an example for our children and those around us. Are there prayer needs that we have today? Can we give something out of our abundance that will bless others? Is there a frown on our face or a smile showing the joy of the Lord? Is the Lord speaking to us out of His Word at this moment?

Step 131

• •

The wise in heart will receive commands, but a prating fool
will fall. He who walks with integrity walks securely, but he
who perverts his ways will become known. He who winks with
the eye causes trouble, but a prating fool will fall. The mouth
of the righteous is a well of life, but violence covers the mouth
of the wicked. Hatred stirs up strife, but love covers all sins.
—Proverbs 10:8–12 (NKJV)

We are those who walk in honesty and integrity. We know they are
elements of wisdom and maturity. This is the place of safety and
security.

We will keep our hearts pure, and out of our mouths will come
words of truth. What we say is evidence of what is in our hearts.
It begins with keeping our thoughts in check. When we guard our
tongues, we build up rather than tear down.

All that the Lord has done for us has come from love. Because
He first loved us, we strive to love others unconditionally. We are
commanded to love God and to love others as we love ourselves.
The opposite of love is anger and hate. It is in that place that we lose
control and do irreparable harm to others and to ourselves. Both
emotions have power, and one can cancel the other. When we love,
we are in tune with heaven.

Step 132

The rich man's wealth is his strong city; the destruction of the
poor is their poverty. The labor of the righteous leads to life,
the wages of the wicked to sin.
He who keeps instruction is in the way of life,
but he who refuses correction goes astray.
In the multitude of words sin is not lacking,
but he who restrains his lips is wise.
The tongue of the righteous is choice silver;
the heart of the wicked is worth little.
The lips of the righteous feed many,
but fools die for lack of wisdom.
—Proverbs 10:15–17, 19–21 (NKJV)

If God has prospered you to some level of wealth, then give Him
thanks. If God has provided a good job, a good boss to work for
and a successful environment, then give Him praise. If there is lack,
worry, and striving for these things, then seek the Lord in prayer. It
is God's plan for us to have some measure of prosperity and not be
bogged down in solving financial problems.

It is God's plan for us to have enough money to pay the bills and
have some left over to give away. A generous heart and a peaceful soul
is God's best for us. That is the place we want to get to, and He will
instruct us on how to get there.

Complaining and babbling about life's problems gets us
nowhere. Are the words we speak reflective of negative thoughts or
the result of a deep trust in God? A few well-chosen words can open
the doors to a rich life. People are listening to what we say and how
we are allowing God to work in our lives.

Step 133

• •

> The blessing of the Lord makes one rich, and He adds no
> sorrow with it. To do evil is like sport to a fool, but a man
> of understanding has wisdom. The fear of the wicked will
> come upon him, and the desire of the righteous will be
> granted. When the whirlwind passes by, the wicked is no
> more, but the righteous has an everlasting foundation.
> —Proverbs 10:22–25 (NKJV)

We may be lacking in some area, but it is God's desire to prosper us
in our finances, heal our bodies, and our relationships. The riches of
the Lord come in many forms and not just in cash money. He will
make us rich in ways that we could never imagine or desire with no
strings attached. The abundance of the Lord is without boundaries.

He will fill us with understanding through His Word and give
us wisdom to apply it. His desire is to encourage and build us up.
Every day with the Lord is a new opportunity for His blessings to be
released upon us. It is through His grace and mercy that our desires
are granted and we can amount to something.

Our past sins have been forgiven and our future is secure. He
has given us the present to seek Him and understand His plan for us.
We are not here to only breathe the air and take up space. Each one
of us is valuable in God's sight. We are the apple of His eye. If we are
willing, He will use us to do mighty works in His kingdom.

Step 134

● ●

The fear of the Lord prolongs days, but the years of the wicked will be shortened. The hope of the righteous will be gladness, but the expectation of the wicked will perish. The way of the Lord is strength for the upright, but destruction will come to the workers of iniquity. The righteous will never be removed, but the wicked will not inhabit the earth. The mouth of the righteous brings forth wisdom, but the perverse tongue will be cut out. The lips of the righteous know what is acceptable, but the mouth of the wicked what is perverse.
—Proverbs 10:27–32 (NKJV)

We are the righteousness of the Lord which are favored and blessed by Him. Because we reverence and love the Lord, our days are lengthened and prolonged. Sickness, disease, and accident shall have no way with us.

It is in the presence of the Lord we experience joy and gladness. We expect to wake up each day in His care and security. No matter what life brings our way we are ready and prepared to handle it.

Our strength and hope is in the Lord; He is our protection. We will trust and depend on the Lord to get us through each adverse circumstance. We will not fear what the devil might send our way; he will have no way with us.

Because God's Word is in us, we will only speak truth and encouragement. Out of pure hearts will our mouths speak. Our will is the will of God, and His ways will become our ways.

Step 135

• •

> Dishonest scales are an abomination to the Lord, but a just
> weight is His delight. When pride comes, then comes shame;
> but with the humble is wisdom. The integrity of the upright
> will guide them, but the perversity of the unfaithful will
> destroy them. Riches do not profit in the day of wrath, but
> righteousness delivers from death. The righteousness of the
> blameless will direct his way aright, but the wicked will fall
> by his own wickedness. The righteousness of the upright will
> deliver them, but the unfaithful will be caught by their lust.
> —Proverbs 11:1–6 (NKJV)

The Lord delights in the integrity of His children. We have taken to
heart a lesson that honesty will guide us on the correct path. It would
be easy and seemingly less painful to lie when accused, but in the
end, truth is the best answer.

The result of pride is shame. When we realize that we have
acted in a puffed-up manner, then the error is revealed and shame
comes. Thankfully, Jesus has taken all our shame and guilt so that we
can walk free and unburdened. Integrity and humility are refreshing
to the soul.

There are some things that money can't buy. Righteousness is
one of them; it is a free gift from God. It has the power to keep us
out of trouble and on the right path. By receiving Jesus Christ as our
Lord and Savior, we became the righteousness of God, and our lives
were changed forever! Halleluiah!

Step 136

● ●

When a wicked man dies, his expectation will perish, and the hope of the unjust perishes. The righteous is delivered from trouble, and it comes to the wicked instead. The hypocrite with his mouth destroys his neighbor, but through knowledge the righteous will be delivered. When it goes well with the righteous, the city rejoices; and when the wicked perish, there is jubilation. By the blessing of the upright the city is exalted, but it is overthrown by the mouth of the wicked.
—Proverbs 11:7–11 (NKJV)

We have a hope and an expectation that unbelievers do not have. We are secure in the present and sure of our future in heaven. We know that when our last day arrives, we will be carried out of this life into a glorious party with the saints. And we will be perfect and complete with no hint or stain of sin.

There is power in our words. Let us be very careful in what comes out of our mouths. People will accuse and condemn us in error. They are just trying to cover their own inadequacies, but we will not be moved off the rock of Jesus.

It is our desire that the city where we live be immersed in the power of the Holy Spirit. The lost will be so moved that they repent and give their lives to Jesus. We pray for a mighty move of salvation and righteousness in the neighborhood where we live. Let Jesus be Lord over our city and His presence felt by all who reside or visit here.

Step 137

• •

> He who is devoid of wisdom despises his neighbor, but a man
> of understanding holds his peace. A talebearer reveals secrets,
> but he who is of a faithful spirit conceals a matter. Where
> there is no counsel, the people fall; But in the multitude of
> counselors there is safety. He who is surety for a stranger
> will suffer, but one who hates being surety is secure.
> —Proverbs 11:12–15 (NKJV)

The wise know when to speak and when to hold their tongues. We have to realize that sometimes words spoken are helpful and encouraging. We always have to be on guard that what is said is not gossip. At other times, it would have been best to just be quiet because what was spoken did more harm than good. The Holy Spirit is our guide when it comes to speaking into a situation. He will give us the right words to use at just the right time.

The body of Christ is wise to listen to good counsel. Look at a person's life and listen to what they say to know if it is good counsel. We all have opinions and good ideas that may not be God's ideas. A good counselor is not always the first to speak or one who has a lot to say. But those few words at just the right moment can change a situation and move the church in the right direction.

At times, we are faced with situations where the decision must be made to loan or not. Cosigning a loan may seem like an innocent choice when it was not God's idea at all. God's people are generous givers. There are times when just giving something is better than loaning it.

Step 138

• •

A gracious woman retains honor, but ruthless men retain riches.
The merciful man does good for his own soul, but he who is
cruel troubles his own flesh. The wicked man does deceptive
work, but he who sows righteousness will have a sure reward.
As righteousness leads to life, so he who pursues evil pursues
it to his own death. Those who are of a perverse heart are an
abomination to the Lord, but the blameless in their ways are
His delight. Though they join forces, the wicked will not go
unpunished; but the posterity of the righteous will be delivered.
—Proverbs 11:16–21 (NKJV)

It is better to be known for honor than for riches. Honor, virtue,
integrity, and righteousness are all outstanding qualities of Christian
character and are health to our bodies. It is desirable to have enough
money to pay the bills and a little left over to give away. But to desire
money just to be wealthy is not our goal because our reward is in
heaven.

Mercy and righteousness are a good combination. God had
mercy upon us when He made us righteous. So out of that righteousness, let us be merciful to our fellow man and let us be a delight
unto the Lord.

To be in right relationship and position with God is essential
to life in the Spirit. Because of the sacrifice of Jesus on the cross and
His resurrection, we have been made righteous with the Father. As
unbelievers view our lives, may they see evidence of the righteousness
of God in us.

Step 139

••••••••••••••••••••••••••••••••••

The desire of the righteous is only good, but the expectation of the wicked is wrath. There is one who scatters, yet increases more; and there is one who withholds more than is right, but it leads to poverty. The generous soul will be made rich, and he who waters will also be watered himself. The people will curse him who withholds grain, but blessing will be on the head of him who sells it.
—Proverbs 11:23–26 (NKJV)

The generous person blesses others and is blessed in return. This person looks for ways to benefit someone else out of his abundance. Take an inventory, do we have something that we are not using that someone else could use?

There is a spiritual principle that is attached to giving. The more we give away, the more we are blessed. To withhold a gift out of fear of loss deprives us of a blessing. When we give into the work of the kingdom, God multiplies and gives back to us.

There are needs in our area of responsibility that we may not be seeing. We have to look around and maybe ask some questions. If we listen carefully, we will hear of lack. We may not be able to fill the need but may be able to help in some small way.

Not all wants or needs have to be filled with a gift. If there is considerable value involved, then a fair price can be offered. That act of generosity can be a real blessing to someone in need.

Step 140

• •

He who earnestly seeks good finds favor, but trouble will come
to him who seeks evil. He who trusts in his riches will fall, but
the righteous will flourish like foliage. He who troubles his own
house will inherit the wind, and the fool will be servant to the
wise of heart. The fruit of the righteous is a tree of life, and he
who wins souls is wise. If the righteous will be recompensed
on the earth, how much more the ungodly and the sinner.
—Proverbs 11:27–31 (NKJV)

Goodness and God's favor go together. God blesses and favors the
worshipper, the giver, and the soul-winner. God is gracious. He is
full of loving-kindness and goodness. Those who seek to be more like
Him will find his goodness.

We will not trust in our riches which can be gone in an instant.
A thief can steal our savings, an investment can go bad, and the economy may sour. But the wealth of the Lord continues to matriculate
and grow.

Divorce, adultery, alcoholism, separation, or division can
destroy a home and break up a family. The father and mother who
value a good home will do all in their power to keep it intact. God
blesses the home and family that seek Him.

We will do the work of the Lord, whatever He asks us to do.
We do not seek great recompense on earth; our reward is in heaven.
What a joy it is to be used mightily by the Lord to further His kingdom on earth.

Step 141

• •

> Whoever loves instruction loves knowledge, but he who hates
> correction is stupid. A good man obtains favor from the Lord,
> but a man of wicked intentions He will condemn. A man is
> not established by wickedness, but the root of the righteous
> cannot be moved. An excellent wife is the crown of her husband,
> but she who causes shame is like rottenness in his bones. The
> thoughts of the righteous are right, but the counsels of the
> wicked are deceitful. The words of the wicked are, "Lie in wait
> for blood," but the mouth of the upright will deliver them.
> —Proverbs 12:1–6 (NKJV)

The Lord's instruction corrects error in our ways. More learning and knowledge lead to wisdom. A heart full of God's wisdom cannot be shaken. His favor surrounds the righteous.

The secret to a happy marriage is for both partners to love God first. God's love has the power to strengthen a relationship. That love trickles down into love for our spouse. Examine a divorce, separation, or broken relationship and notice the love of God is missing.

Out of a heart set apart for the Lord come right thoughts. With right thinking, correct speaking is generated. A rotten heart contaminates thinking and speech. The righteous operate from a pure and renewed heart.

Step 142

The wicked are overthrown and are no more, but the house of
the righteous will stand. A man will be commended according
to his wisdom, but he who is of a perverse heart will be despised.
Better is the one who is slighted but has a servant, than he
who honors himself but lacks bread. A righteous man regards
the life of his animal, but the tender mercies of the wicked
are cruel. He who tills his land will be satisfied with bread,
but he who follows frivolity is devoid of understanding.
—Proverbs 12:7–11 (NKJV)

Natural disasters come upon all of us, but the righteous will not fear
or become hopeless. We have a relationship with our Lord that cannot be broken. His plan and promises sustain us so that we have a
legacy to pass on to others.

We will walk by faith in the wisdom that God has provided in
His Word. We will not worry about tomorrow because today has
enough challenges for us. But we will not become complacent instead
humble ourselves under the mighty hand of God. We welcome the
mystery of not having all the answers and of not knowing what the
future might bring.

Persecution, criticism, and mockery will come, but we will not
be shaken. We will put our hand to the plow and welcome each new
day. We thank God for the job we have and the provision that He has
provided. We will care for what we have and put it to good use. Each
day, we are given is a blessing from the Lord who provides all things.

Step 143

• •

The wicked covet the catch of evil men, but the root of the righteous yields fruit. The wicked is ensnared by the transgression of his lips, but the righteous will come through trouble. A man will be satisfied with good by the fruit of his mouth, and the recompense of a man's hands will be rendered to him. The way of a fool is right in his own eyes, but he who heeds counsel is wise. A fool's wrath is known at once, but a prudent man covers shame.
—Proverbs 12:12–16 (NKJV)

The things of the ungodly may glitter and look appealing, but they have no real value. The Holy Spirit will direct us to the things God wants us to pursue. He will meet all our needs in Christ Jesus.

We are the people who have pure and circumcised hearts. Out of that new heart comes the right thoughts and words, and then from these hearts set apart to the Lord is a harvest of actions.

We have to guard our tongues because we can easily bring trouble into our lives by what we say. Wrong thoughts and words lead to sin. There is power in the tongue to release good or evil into our lives or the lives of others.

It is foolish to think we have all the right answers. It's wise to be open to prayer from a brother or sister in the Lord. God will use others to speak into our lives if we are humble and willing to receive it. We are sometimes blind to what is best for us in a particular situation. Another set of eyes can see what is hidden from our view.

Step 144

He who speaks truth declares righteousness, but a false witness,
deceit. There is one who speaks like the piercings of a sword, but
the tongue of the wise promotes health. The truthful lip shall
be established forever, but a lying tongue is but for a moment.
Deceit is in the heart of those who devise evil, but counselors of
peace have joy. No grave trouble will overtake the righteous, but
the wicked shall be filled with evil. Lying lips are an abomination
to the Lord, but those who deal truthfully are His delight.
—Proverbs 12:17–22 (NKJV)

We are those who use our voices to speak truth. It would be so easy to
tell a little white lie to sooth our bruised ego. An exaggeration could
build up our image of ourselves for a moment. And maybe we try to
impress someone by stretching the truth. But our emphasis will be
on telling the truth to the best of our ability.

We mix gentleness with the truth because sometimes truth
hurts. Our words are to be soft, warm, and encouraging. As we speak
in this manner, it brings health to our soul.

A spoken truth is solid and established. It lasts and cannot be
shaken. Our truthful words are to bring peace and joy. Evil hurtful
speech brings darkness and trouble.

God's spoken truth is a delight to our ears and to the hearing of others. There is power in His revelation of truth. Let us be
pure mouthpieces of God's Word that can change circumstances and
attitudes.

Step 145

● ●

A prudent man conceals knowledge, but the heart of fools proclaims foolishness. The hand of the diligent will rule, but the lazy man will be put to forced labor. Anxiety in the heart of man causes depression, but a good word makes it glad. The righteous should choose his friends carefully, for the way of the wicked leads them astray. The lazy man does not roast what he took in hunting, but diligence is man's precious possession. In the way of righteousness is life, and in its pathway there is no death.
—Proverbs 12:23–28 (NKJV)

Sometimes it is wise to not speak into a situation right away. That gives a little more time to access what's going on and then address it.

Anxiety and worry are enemies of our peace and joy. They are unproductive emotions that displace the ones that are good for our soul. Worry never solved anything but created worthless thoughts. Positive and comforting words stir a glad heart.

The ways and words of the unbeliever can steal our joy. We realize quickly we have very little in common with their conversation. We want to share the love of Jesus with them, and often they are put off. We have set our course upon Jesus and will not go astray.

We have chosen a lifestyle that leads to eternal life in heaven. We have seen and experienced the darkness and only want the light. Our pathway is charted, and with the help of the Holy Spirit, we will not veer off it.

Step 146

● ●

A wise son heeds his father's instruction, but a scoffer does
not listen to rebuke. A man shall eat well by the fruit of his
mouth, but the soul of the unfaithful feeds on violence. He
who guards his mouth preserves his life, but he who opens
wide his lips shall have destruction. The soul of a lazy man
desires, and has nothing; but the soul of the diligent shall be
made rich. A righteous man hates lying, but a wicked man is
loathsome and comes to shame. Righteousness guards him
whose way is blameless, but wickedness overthrows the sinner.
—Proverbs 13:1–6 (NKJV)

Most of us wish that we had listened to the good counsel of our parents. And as parents, we wish that we had provided better guidance
for our children, and that they would have listened to it. Alas, we did
the best we could, and we can't go back and change the past. And
with the guidance and counsel of the Holy Spirit, we have an opportunity to heed His instruction.

If there is any laziness in us, then we ask the Lord to remove it.
When we ask, we know we receive. Our time on earth is short, and
we want to be faithful to what God has given us, called us to be and
to do.

We are the righteous that spend each day seeking what the
Lord wants to show us and give us. We receive forgiveness for having
strayed from the course but strive to stay on the straight and narrow
path. We walk in the Spirit and feed on the bread of heaven.

Step 147

● ●

There is one who makes himself rich, yet has nothing; and one who
makes himself poor, yet has great riches. The ransom of a man's
life is his riches, but the poor does not hear rebuke. The light of
the righteous rejoices, but the lamp of the wicked will be put out.
—Proverbs 13:7–9 (NKJV)

There are those who strive for wealth, and when they have it, it is not
enough. Riches do not satisfy, yet the love of Jesus, eternal salvation,
and hope for the future are desirable. Accumulation of money and
things leaves one empty and longing for more. There is a hunger
inside of us that cannot be filled by this world.

Wealth that is gained selfishly brings waste, lavish living, and
fear. It's easy to criticize the rich person who spends excessively on
himself but easier to compliment the one who accumulates to give
away. There is a wealthy mind-set that gains riches honestly to be
given away and for the benefit of others. Giving does not bring fear
but inspires us to look for the needs of others and do our best to help
fill them.

In God's presence is love, joy, and peace. When we have His
light inside of us, we cannot behave selfishly; we want to share it with
others. And when we join collectively with other believers, that light
grows even brighter. The light of the righteous cannot be snuffed out
because its source is from heaven.

Step 148

He who despises the word will be destroyed, but he who fears
the commandment will be rewarded. The law of the wise is
a fountain of life, to turn one away from the snares of death.
Good understanding gains favor, but the way of the unfaithful
is hard. Every prudent man acts with knowledge, but a fool
lays open his folly. A wicked messenger falls into trouble, but
a faithful ambassador brings health. Poverty and shame will
come to him who disdains correction, but he who regards a
rebuke will be honored. A desire accomplished is sweet to the
soul, but it is an abomination to fools to depart from evil.
—Proverbs 13:13–19 (NKJV)

The wisdom of the Lord is a fountain of life. By taking it to heart,
we can avoid some of the pitfalls of life. When we are steeped in the
word, we gain favor with God and with man. When we look into the
Word of God, we think, speak, and act correctly.

We are God's ambassadors for His kingdom on earth. God's
will to be done on earth as it is in heaven is through willing vessels
like you and me. We are to dispel worry and fear by bringing words
of healing.

When our will and God's will line up, it is sweet to the soul.
Poverty, shame, and sickness come to those who ignore the strength
and wisdom of the Lord. We enjoy a rich and pleasant fellowship
with the Lord when we abide in His presence.

Step 149

● ●

He who walks with wise men will be wise, but the companion
of fools will be destroyed. Evil pursues sinners, but to the
righteous, good shall be repaid. A good man leaves an
inheritance to his children's children, but the wealth of the
sinner is stored up for the righteous. Much food is in the
fallow ground of the poor, and for lack of justice there is waste.
He who spares his rod hates his son, but he who loves him
disciplines him promptly. The righteous eats to the satisfying
of his soul, but the stomach of the wicked shall be in want.
—Proverbs 13:20–25 (NKJV)

We are those who associate ourselves with wise people and heed their
counsel. It is also our desire to help those who make foolish mistakes,
but we will not be drawn into their misery.

A good parent disciplines his child for as long as the offspring
will listen. God disciplines us out of love and sets the example for
earthly parents. Without correction, we are left to our own devices,
and that is a poor way to live.

God has blessed us in multiple ways so that we might prosper
and have an abundance. We are not to bury our money out of fear of
loss. Money put to good use makes more money to be used wisely in
the kingdom. We are not to squander what He has provided and to
use it wisely. One of the ways we do that is to leave an inheritance for
our family and for our grandchildren.

Step 150

The wise woman builds her house, but the foolish pulls it down with her hands. He who walks in his uprightness fears the Lord, but he who is perverse in his ways despises Him. In the mouth of a fool is a rod of pride, but the lips of the wise will preserve them. Where no oxen are, the trough is clean; but much increase comes by the strength of an ox. A faithful witness does not lie, but a false witness will utter lies.
—Proverbs 14:1–5 (NKJV)

The wise woman establishes a safe and godly home. It is organized, orderly, and clean. Her mark is upon its furnishings, and it is creatively designed. The Christian home is a peaceful sanctuary and fit for raising children in the Lord. We may not have achieved all of this, but it is the standard we strive for.

Uprightness is the way of the Christian. The Word of the Lord is his guide along the way. Out of his mouth come words of truth, and they are delivered in humility. He speaks truth in the courtroom of life. Each day, he praises the Lord and honors and respects the God of his salvation.

Each one of us has been gifted and talented in a special way. We are to use the unique set of qualities to build and create. It is to be done by integrity, creativity, and excellence. Our bills are paid by the fruit of our labor. God blesses those who work unto Him.

Step 151

• •

A scoffer seeks wisdom and does not find it, but knowledge
is easy to him who understands. Go from the presence of
a foolish man, when you do not perceive in him the lips of
knowledge. The wisdom of the prudent is to understand
his way, but the folly of fools is deceit. Fools mock at sin,
but among the upright there is favor. The heart knows its
own bitterness, and a stranger does not share its joy.
—Proverbs 14:6–10 (NKJV)

We are on a continuous search for God's wisdom. Our hearts are
open to the Word and to revelation from the Lord. We will seek to
hear what the Holy Spirit is saying and see what He is showing us.

When we share the good news with an unbeliever, it is not
always received with the same enthusiasm that it is given. We never
know whether we are planting or watering, but we are to be faithful
in the process.

We will continue to walk in the way that God has shown us
regardless of the circumstances or what unbelievers might say. With
the help and strength of the Holy Spirit, we will strive to stay out of
sin. We know there is favor in a closer walk with Jesus.

The road of life is full of ups and downs. At times, we fall into
bitterness, sadness, and despair. But that place is only a visit and only
a small part of our journey. It's the joy of the Lord where we dwell,
spend our time, and find our strength.

Step 152

● ●

> The house of the wicked will be overthrown, but the tent of
> the upright will flourish. There is a way that seems right to
> a man, but its end is the way of death. Even in laughter the
> heart may sorrow, and the end of mirth may be grief. The
> backslider in heart will be filled with his own ways, but a
> good man will be satisfied from above. The simple believes
> every word, but the prudent considers well his steps.
> —Proverbs 14:11–15 (NKJV)

We will make our way through choices that are guided by the Holy
Spirit. The days of floundering by trying to satisfy our earthly desires
are past. We are on a path that leads to heaven and a face-to-face
encounter with Jesus, our Savior.

Our emotional outburst may not make a lot of sense. Sometimes
we will laugh in the midst of sadness and cry with joy. In the Spirit
is a place that transcends the five senses and human emotions. We
march and dance to a different drummer.

There is often conflict between what the Holy Spirit is saying
and our own spirit is desiring. Who will we listen to and obey? Our
own confused and misguided way can lead to backsliding. Hearing
and obeying the Holy Spirit keeps us on the right path.

Joy and satisfaction with the direction we are going comes from
yielding to God's will. Jesus has given us this day as a present to be
opened and enjoyed. There is no going back to the old ways of selfishness and self-seeking pleasures.

Step 153

● ●

A wise man fears and departs from evil, but a fool rages and is
self-confident. A quick-tempered man acts foolishly, and a man
of wicked intentions is hated. The simple inherit folly, but the
prudent are crowned with knowledge. The evil will bow before the
good, and the wicked at the gates of the righteous. The poor man
is hated even by his own neighbor, but the rich has many friends.
—Proverbs 14:16–20 (NKJV)

We who love the Lord do not take temptation and sin lightly. The
devil goes about roaring like a hungry lion seeking who he might
devour. Paul warns us not to give in to evil but to call on the name of
Jesus, and the devil must flee from us. We also have the Holy Spirit
that warns us when sin is near and to avoid it. We never get so sure
of ourselves to think we cannot be tempted.

We understand the power of anger and how it can consume
us. It is our desire to seek peace and understanding in all situations.
Anger is an emotion that can eat away at us and eventually consume
us. So we look for a way out that results in patience, peace, and joy.
With the power of the Holy Spirit, we will find that door and walk
right through it.

The poor man is often misunderstood by those around him.
His attempts to climb out of poverty are difficult and a struggle.
Surely being poor is not the desire of his life. We who are rich are
called by God to help the poor as much as we can. The poor will
always be with us but praise be to God for those who successfully
leave poverty behind.

Step 154

• •

In the fear of the Lord there is strong confidence, and His children will have a place of refuge. The fear of the Lord is a fountain of life, to turn one away from the snares of death. In a multitude of people is a king's honor, but in the lack of people is the downfall of a prince. He who is slow to wrath has great understanding, but he who is impulsive exalts folly. A sound heart is life to the body, but envy is rottenness to the bones.
—Proverbs 14:26–30 (NKJV)

In the presence of the Lord, there is strong confidence. When we honor, respect, and reverence the Lord, there is a confidence that is released in us. We know we are loved and have an inheritance from the Father. We go about our day feeling safe and secure. The Holy Spirit has been assigned to look after us and care for us.

We have tapped into a source of life that will carry us into eternity. We have been delivered from the pit of hell. We are no longer in the devil's camp but now are part of God's glorious kingdom.

Anger and envy have no part in us. These two emotions steal health from our bodies and keep our focus off of God. But our hearts are at peace knowing the Holy Spirit is nearby. Out of a pure heart spring the wholesome and important issues of life. We manifest joy, peace, and love out of a heart dedicated unto the Lord.

Step 155

●●●●●●●●●●●●●●●●●●●●●●●●●●●●●●●●

He who oppresses the poor reproaches his Maker, but he who honors Him has mercy on the needy. The wicked is banished in his wickedness, but the righteous has a refuge in his death. Wisdom rests in the heart of him who has understanding, but what is in the heart of fools is made known. Righteousness exalts a nation, but sin is a reproach to any people. The king's favor is toward a wise servant, but his wrath is against him who causes shame.
—Proverbs 14:31–35 (NKJV)

Let us not be a people who criticize or disparage the poor. We could very easily be in the same position or worse with a change in our circumstances. We are to take every opportunity to assist and help those less fortunate than ourselves. It pleases God when we do our part to aid the poor. If we ask, He will show us what we are to do.

We are secure in knowing that God is looking out for us, and that we have a home in heaven. There is wisdom in knowing that God desires to use our gifts and abilities to further His kingdom. Collectively we as the body of Christ raise up our community and our nation before God.

It is a wise leader who recognizes the presence of Christians in the community. We bring a heavenly understanding to each situation that is a benefit to others. It is a foolish leader who ignores the presence of God and rejects the power of prayer. Yes, we have an inside track to helping solve social problems and the resources to be of assistance.

Step 156

• •

A soft answer turns away wrath, but a harsh word stirs up anger.
The tongue of the wise uses knowledge rightly, but the mouth of
fools pours forth foolishness. The eyes of the Lord are in every
place, keeping watch on the evil and the good. A wholesome
tongue is a tree of life, but perverseness in it breaks the spirit.
—Proverbs 15:1–4 (NKJV)

The Spirit-filled believer knows when to speak up and when to be
quiet. In an argument or verbal attack, the Christian does not raise
his voice but answers with a soft reply. His words come from a place
of peace and humility. The Holy Spirit will give us the right words to
speak in a difficult situation.

The student of the Word of God studies them and stores them
in his heart. More and more the wisdom of the Word becomes a reservoir of knowledge in our hearts. It is from that place that we think,
speak, and act.

We serve an omniscient God who is all seeing, all wise, and
all knowing. It is foolish for us to think we can hide anything from
Him. We realize that He sees the darkness and the light in us. Receive
forgiveness for the sins and walk forever in the blessings.

There is power in the tongue; it can build up or tear down.
We are to speak words of encouragement and edification. When we
speak in this way, we also build ourselves up and avoid the contami-
nation of wrong speaking.

Step 157

• •

> A merry heart makes a cheerful countenance, but by sorrow
> of the heart the spirit is broken. The heart of him who has
> understanding seeks knowledge, but the mouth of fools feeds
> on foolishness. All the days of the afflicted are evil, but he who
> is of a merry heart has a continual feast. Better is a little with
> the fear of the Lord, than great treasure with trouble. Better is
> a dinner of herbs where love is, than a fatted calf with hatred.
> —Proverbs 15:13–17 (NKJV)

A cheerful countenance begins with a happy and contented heart. Sadness and sorrow can bring a person down and prevent a joyful heart. We can't afford to spend much time in those emotions because life is too short. We allow the Holy Spirit to comfort us and lift us up. A smile has the power to change the atmosphere.

Time spent in meditation and prayer can enlighten us to our mood. We seek understanding and relief from whatever is dragging us down. It's time to stop wallowing in our sorrow and join the feast of merry hearts. God will heal and strengthen a broken heart. He knows everything about us and has given us a solution for our problem.

There is great riches and contentment in fellowship with the Lord. He desires our time, attention, and intimacy. He hears and answers our prayers because of His great love for us. There is wealth in our relationship with the Lord and with fellow believers. It's time to raise our voices in praise and worship.

Step 158

• •

A wrathful man stirs up strife, but he who is slow to anger
allays contention. The way of the lazy man is like a hedge of
thorns, but the way of the upright is a highway. A wise son
makes a father glad, but a foolish man despises his mother.
Folly is joy to him who is destitute of discernment, but a man
of understanding walks uprightly. Without counsel, plans go
awry, but in the multitude of counselors they are established.
—Proverbs 15:18–22 (NKJV)

Strife and contention spoil a marriage, family, and working relationships. It takes godly wisdom to see the damage that these two struggles bring to a relationship. It is better to slow down and let the
situation cool before allowing a fire to start.

We are the righteous of God who walk the highway. It is a narrow road that the lazy or foolish despise. But we see the value in
letting the Holy Spirit be our guide through the jungle of confusion
and darkness.

We are all fortunate to have a mother who birthed us. However,
not all enjoyed a healthy or happy family life. For those who did
come from a good home, we thank the moms and dads who sacri-
ficed and nurtured us.

Churches need a vision and direction from God to move forward. Then it's important to have leaders who can implement the
purpose and plan for the church. A church struggles to move ahead
if there is disagreement and division within it.

Step 159

● ●

A man has joy by the answer of his mouth, and a word spoken
in due season, how good it is! The way of life winds upward
for the wise, that he may turn away from hell below. The Lord
will destroy the house of the proud, but He will establish the
boundary of the widow. The thoughts of the wicked are an
abomination to the Lord, but the words of the pure are pleasant.
He who is greedy for gain troubles his own house, but he who
hates bribes will live. The heart of the righteous studies how
to answer, but the mouth of the wicked pours forth evil.
—Proverbs 15:23–28 (NKJV)

A word of joy is spoken from a joyful heart. As we see others built up
by what we say, we too are lifted up. God wants to use us as encouragement to others. But we must be willing and open to hear from
God and then bold to speak out. A word from God is powerful and
uplifting.

Ever since we gave our hearts to the Lord, our lives have taken
an upturn. Worries and shame from the past have diminished. We
can hold our heads up, and there is a spring in our step. Troubles and
difficulties still come around, but we have a whole new attitude and
way of dealing with them. We have a hope in the future that continues to take us higher.

Words spoken without the Holy Spirit's influence are just advice,
hearsay, and gossip. They don't carry any weight and are here today
and gone tomorrow. Carefully chosen words bathed in the light and
wisdom of the Lord are golden and lasting.

Step 160

● ●

The Lord is far from the wicked, but He hears the prayer of the righteous. The light of the eyes rejoices the heart, and a good report makes the bones healthy. The ear that hears the rebukes of life will abide among the wise He who disdains instruction despises his own soul, but he who heeds rebuke gets understanding. The fear of the Lord is the instruction of wisdom, and before honor is humility.
—Proverbs 15:29–33 (NKJV)

It's good to know that the Lord is near and hears our prayers. Besides hearing, He also answers our prayers. The answer may not come right away or be what we wanted to hear. But God is faithful to listen and speak to us in that still small voice.

When we walk in the light of God's countenance, our hearts are uplifted. We sense the joy of heaven and know that all is well with our souls. The joy and peace of God are health to our flesh and strength to our bones. We desire the good report that says we are healed in our bodies and minds.

We hear the rebukes of life and know that they can hurt us or help us to grow if we abide by them. This is the place where we join others who are growing and maturing. God knows that as we go about this day, we will make mistakes because we are not perfect. We are works in progress doing our best to walk in truth and reverence to God. Humility is our first response which leads to wisdom and honor.

Step 161

The preparations of the heart belong to man, but the answer
of the tongue is from the Lord. All the ways of a man are pure
in his own eyes, but the Lord weighs the spirits. Commit your
works to the Lord, and your thoughts will be established. The
Lord has made all for Himself, yes, even the wicked for the
day of doom. Everyone proud in heart is an abomination to
the Lord; though they join forces, none will go unpunished.
In mercy and truth Atonement is provided for iniquity;
And by the fear of the Lord one departs from evil.
—Proverbs 16:1–6 (NKJV)

We will go through this day as best as we know how. However, it is
our desire for our thoughts to be from the Lord and the words of our
mouths to be guided by the wisdom of the Holy Spirit. We commit
our ways to the Lord because in our own strength we can go astray.

God is the creator of all life, and a discerning eye will see the
hand of the Lord in many things. It is foolish to dismiss the work
of the Lord and to be deceived into thinking that all life is an accident. God has a plan for all of us, and He has clearly outlined it in
His book, the Bible. Just because we are surrounded by unbelievers
doesn't change the truth of God's existence and sovereignty.

To refuse to recognize God is to live in sin. God in His mercy
sent His Son, Jesus, to reveal Himself to us. The death and resurrection of Jesus has made a way for us to be forgiven of all our sins. By
reverencing the Lord, we stay out of the clutches of the evil one.

Step 162

• •

When a man's ways please the Lord, He makes even his
enemies to be at peace with him. Better is a little with
righteousness, than vast revenues without justice. A man's
heart plans his way, but the Lord directs his steps.
—Proverbs 16:7–9 (NKJV)

God's ways are mercy, truth, judgment, and love. When we walk in
the same ways, our enemies are caught off guard. The Bible tells us
to love our enemies even when they are mean to us. When we are
hated without cause, then we are to be patient and understanding.
The truth is we have our faults, and we cannot live this life without
offending others. Judgement belongs to the Lord, so we leave it up to
Him. He sees the whole situation when our eyesight is limited.

When we are well off financially, then we praise God and give.
If we struggle to pay the bills and provide for our families, then we
are to seek God. We know that as we ask, He answers. If we knock,
He will open. Our provision comes from the Lord who has wealth
beyond measure.

The Holy Spirit desires to be in partnership with us. He knows
the plan for our lives, and He sees what is ahead. He will lead us in
the direction we are to go. When our desires line up with God, then
He makes a way for them to be fulfilled. Our primary purpose is to
please God and to be at peace with our fellow man. Only in fellowship with Him can we achieve our purpose and be happy with our
accomplishments. Contentment comes from an intimacy with God
and knowing He is right there with us.

Step 163

●●●●●●●●●●●●●●●●●●●●●●●●●●●●●●●

Divination is on the lips of the king; His mouth must not
transgress in judgment. Honest weights and scales are the Lord's;
All the weights in the bag are His work. It is an abomination
for kings to commit wickedness, for a throne is established by
righteousness. Righteous lips are the delight of kings, and they
love him who speaks what is right. As messengers of death is the
king's wrath, but a wise man will appease it. In the light of the
king's face is life, and his favor is like a cloud of the latter rain.
—Proverbs 16:10–15 (NKJV)

We are kings and priests in God's kingdom. Because we have been
deemed righteous, it is our pleasure to serve the King of kings. In
God's mercy, all our sins have been forgiven, and now we live, move,
and have our being in His grace.

It is our desire to speak what God has placed upon our hearts.
We want to walk in His truth and to announce it to anyone who will
listen. We are not messengers of doom and gloom but bearers of glad
tidings of hope and a glorious future.

Whatever we have gained is a blessing from God. We know He
will open the windows of heaven to anyone who will ask. He knows
just what we need and is the source of all light and life. We are to
express that light and be a source of God's blessings to others. We are
to gift others with a little money, hope, and encouragement.

Step 164

• •

How much better to get wisdom than gold! And to get understanding is to be chosen rather than silver. The highway of the upright is to depart from evil; He who keeps his way preserves his soul. Pride goes before destruction, And a haughty spirit before a fall. Better to be of a humble spirit with the lowly, than to divide the spoil with the proud. He who heeds the word wisely will find good, and whoever trusts in the Lord, happy is he.
—Proverbs 16:16–20 (NKJV)

Since we don't have a lot of gold, it's important to have wisdom to manage what we do have. God has blessed us abundantly, and it's important that we make every dollar count. He will show us when to save and when to spend. The world flashes all kinds of temptation in front of us to entice us to spend foolishly.

The highway of the upright is the road we travel, and He keeps us from the ditches of sin. To think we can operate without the guiding of the Holy Spirit is prideful. In pride, we choose to go it alone and are destined for a fall. It is in humility that we cancel out pride.

When we put our faith and trust in the Lord, that is where we find joy and happiness. We have an Abba Father that loves us and shows it by His grace. Whenever we doubt His love or presence, we need only consult His Word and be built-up again. God has good things in store for us and is wanting to reveal them to us.

Step 165

● ●

The wise in heart will be called prudent, and sweetness of the lips
increases learning. Understanding is a wellspring of life to him who
has it. But the correction of fools is folly. The heart of the wise
teaches his mouth, and adds learning to his lips. Pleasant words are
like a honeycomb, sweetness to the soul and health to the bones.
—Proverbs 16:21–24 (NKJV)

We are the wise in our hearts who are not satisfied with what we
know but have a hunger to learn more. We are also on the alert for
correction that increases our understanding. We listen to teachers
who also have wisdom to give and do it in a gentle manner that is
easy to receive and digest. The Holy Spirit is one such teacher.

Our hearts are reservoirs that desire to be filled to the rim.
Godly wisdom and truth cause us to grow and mature. We have a
capacity to learn that will be continued beyond our earthly lives. To
imagine being filled with heavenly knowledge boggles the mind. Let
us speak with the wisdom and truth of God.

Words spoken from a gentle and humble heart are powerful.
Those words increase understanding, calm the emotions, and set us
up for good decisions. Words of doubt and hopelessness are harmful
to our health. Sickness and disease feed on the negative. But positive
words of encouragement are strength to our physical bodies.

Step 166

• •

The silver-haired head is a crown of glory, if it is found in the way of righteousness. He who is slow to anger is better than the mighty, and he who rules his spirit than he who takes a city. The lot is cast into the lap, but its every decision is from the Lord.
—Proverbs 16:31–33 (NKJV)

We might think that gray hair is not a crown but only a sign of getting old and slowing down. But for many, the years of gray hair may number more than the days of youth. The senior years can be the best times of our lives. There is a sense that life is fragile and short, and that good health is a blessing from the Lord. It is in our righteousness with God that our remaining years can be extremely productive.

Two things the mature person enjoys are peace and joy. It is in that place that we are slow to anger and humble. Our circumstances no longer have control over us, but we are in control of them. We draw on the knowledge of Jesus within us and the presence of the Holy Spirit all around us. We don't have to go through this life alone; God is with us.

As an older person, we have a legacy of skills and experience. We know our God-given gifts and talents. There is an overwhelming awareness of eternal life, and that heaven is real. We have a confidence and hope that unbelievers lack.

Everything we need has been placed within us, and with the help of the Holy Spirit, it can be drawn out. God has equipped us for the journey ahead. We are not here to just breathe and take up space. His plan and purpose is to use all that we are for furthering His kingdom here on earth. Praise the Lord!

Step 167

● ●

Better is a dry morsel with quietness, than a house full of feasting
with strife. A wise servant will rule over a son who causes shame,
and will share an inheritance among the brothers.
The refining pot is for silver and the furnace for gold,
but the Lord tests the hearts.
Children's children are the crown of old men,
and the glory of children is their father.
—Proverbs 17:1–3, 6 (NKJV)

Strife is not welcome in the home; it steals peace and quietness. The
home is to be a sanctuary from the cares of the world and a place of
rest and refreshing. It is better to have a modest home with peace
than a palace of confusion and strife. What a blessing when husband
and wife love each other and together rule over the home. Their children are to love, honor, and respect their parents.

This life will sometimes challenge us to our limits. But each
difficulty and problem is overcome with the help of the Holy Spirit
who purifies us. God looks on the inside of us and evaluates our
hearts. We might not look like much on the outside, but a pure heart
is a blessing to others and to God. We are pure gold and silver to the
Lord because we are made in His image.

Our earnest desire is to leave a legacy to our children and grandchildren. It is our hope that our offspring give their hearts to the
Lord. We know they will make mistakes and won't always listen to
us. However, if the Lord rules over their home, we can expect a good
outcome.

Step 168

• •

A present is a precious stone in the eyes of its possessor;
Wherever he turns, he prospers.
Rebuke is more effective for a wise man
than a hundred blows on a fool.
Let a man meet a bear robbed of her cubs,
rather than a fool in his folly.
The beginning of strife is like releasing water;
Therefore, stop contention before a quarrel starts.
A friend loves at all times,
and a brother is born for adversity.
—Proverbs 17:8, 10, 12, 14, 17 (NKJV)

We appreciate a good gift and the giver. We see value in a gift and are thankful. The greatest gift we have received is the Lord, Jesus Christ. Because of Christ in us, we are wealthy beyond measure.

As a Christian, it is easy to be shunned and laughed at. It is a life of trials and tribulation, but we are able to learn from our mistakes and grow. Correction from the Lord is welcomed and received.

When we find ourselves in an escalating situation, we know it's better not to throw fuel on the fire. There are things we say and do that will offend people. We let silly criticism roll off of us and do not seek retribution. We will avoid foolish arguments and contention whenever possible.

God's love is in us just waiting to come out. Let us be known as Christians who love others unconditionally just as Christ loves us. The qualities of love, kindness, and goodness are to be first place in our lives.

Step 169

∙ ∙

A merry heart does good, like medicine,
but a broken spirit dries the bones.
Wisdom is in the sight of him who has understanding,
but the eyes of a fool are on the ends of the earth.
He who has knowledge spares his words,
and a man of understanding is of a calm spirit.
—Proverbs 17:22, 24, 27 (NKJV)

A joyful heart lifts the spirit and heals the mind and body. A spirit in turmoil agitates the soul, and the chemistry of the body is disrupted. From that sickness and disease are given entrance to steal our health.

Knowledge and understanding are assets to the Christian. But those alone will not keep us from making poor decisions. It is only when we mix godly wisdom do we overcome our difficulties. We are to operate within our realm of responsibility and not beyond it.

How many times have we wished we could take back the words that were misspoken? Sometimes our mouths are like leaky faucets that won't stop dripping. Our prayer is for the Holy Spirit to guard our tongues and limit our speech.

We are those who are governed by a calm spirit. In connection with the Holy Spirit, there is a peace we can draw on that supersedes our understanding. When we walk in that calm spirit, we influence others and change the atmosphere.

Step 170

The words of a man's mouth are deep waters;
The wellspring of wisdom is a flowing brook.
The name of the Lord is a strong tower;
The righteous run to it and are safe.
The rich man's wealth is his strong city,
and like a high wall in his own esteem.
Before destruction the heart of a man is haughty,
and before honor is humility.
—Proverbs 18:4, 10–12 (NKJV)

Our words are influenced by the Holy Spirit and are wisdom, comfort, and love. The Word of God is in us mixed with life experiences brings forth righteous words. We let those words and thoughts come from a deep place within our spirit.

Our safety and protection come from the Lord. The name of Jesus is in our thoughts and on our tongue. The presence of the Holy Spirit keeps us from danger and covers us in a crisis. As we allow Him to lead us, we avoid all kinds of trouble.

If our neighbor is poor, we will not judge him as inferior but love him unconditionally. Riches are from the Lord, and we appreciate the power and solace they provide us. From our own resources and wealth, we will do our best to meet the need of others. If our neighbor is rich and we are poor, we will not envy him or covet what he has.

We let pride be far from us and draw near to humility. Pride is fool's gold while humility is a precious gem. When we believe ourselves better than others, then we are due for a wake-up call or a downfall. It is always better and more productive to take the lesser position to others.

Step 171

● ●

> The spirit of a man will sustain him in sickness,
> but who can bear a broken spirit?
> The heart of the prudent acquires knowledge,
> and the ear of the wise seeks knowledge.
> A man's gift makes room for him,
> and brings him before great men.
> A man's stomach shall be satisfied from the fruit of his mouth;
> from the produce of his lips he shall be filled.
> —Proverbs 18:14–16, 20 (NKJV)

When our human spirit is connected with the Holy Spirit, we have power over sickness and disease. But if we try to go it on our own, we can fall prey to hopelessness and discouragement. Jesus displayed supernatural power over sickness, and that healing is available to those who will call on it in His name.

It is best to be a good speaker and a good listener. When we pause and listen before speaking, we are more likely to speak correctly into the situation. When we speak wisely, we are more likely to release health and prosperity into our lives and others.

God has given His children gifts and talents. We are to realize what they are and use them wisely. God's gifts, our training, and our skills prepare us for the next big thing God has for us. He has gifted us for a purpose, and He will use those to further His kingdom here on earth. And won't He use that same equipping and more when we get to heaven?

Step 172

• •

Death and life are in the power of the tongue, and those who love
it will eat its fruit. He who finds a wife finds a good thing, and
obtains favor from the Lord. The poor man uses entreaties, but
the rich answers roughly. A man who has friends must himself be
friendly, but there is a friend who sticks closer than a brother.
—Proverbs 18:21–24 (NKJV)

Harmless sayings we speak can invite dangerous consequences. We
can bring curses upon ourselves by what we speak. There is power
in the tongue that must be controlled. Positive words are the goal
of Spirit-filled believers. Negative speech produces spoiled and sour
fruit.

Good husbands and wives are not easy to find on our own. We
need the guidance of the Holy Spirit to select a suitable mate. There
is much to be said about the wrong choice and a high price to pay.
But joy and happiness are available to the couple blessed by God.

The pleas of the poor are to be obeyed with a little money when
possible. It is by the grace of God that we are not on the street begging bread. It could so easily be us who are poor.

A handful of close friends are a blessing from the Lord. To find
good friends, we must be friendly. We need to look around us and
see if we have neglected a friend. A friend is a good find and valuable
like a precious gem. Do we have a friend that needs to hear from us
today with a text or a call?

Step 173

• •

> Better is the poor who walks in his integrity than
> one who is perverse in his lips, and is a fool.
> He who gets wisdom loves his own soul;
> He who keeps understanding will find good.
> The discretion of a man makes him slow to anger,
> and his glory is to overlook a transgression.
> Houses and riches are an inheritance from fathers,
> but a prudent wife is from the Lord.
> —Proverbs 19:1, 8, 11, 14 (NKJV)

The one who is poor but honest has found a good thing. He puts his trust in the Lord and finds his sustenance in the Holy Spirit. His poverty will be replaced by the riches of the Lord. And he will not speak negatively about his situation or against others.

We are those who walk in God's wisdom and allow the Holy Spirit to influence our thoughts, emotions, and decisions. We understand that God's wisdom is superior to the worlds and know that it is the source of our success.

Some might think it's silly to overlook an accusation or a hurt against us. But we don't get caught up in the hate and anger that others display toward us. Let us be those who are slow to anger and resist all forms of retribution.

It is possible to receive an inheritance from a parent or relative. To find a good wife is a gift from God. The richest inheritance is from the grace and mercy of Jesus Christ. The gift of God's Son that takes our sins and gives us eternal life in glory is too great to measure.

Step 174

He who has pity on the poor lends to the Lord,
and He will pay back what he has given.
Chasten your son while there is hope,
and do not set your heart on his destruction.
Listen to counsel and receive instruction,
that you may be wise in your latter days.
There are many plans in a man's heart,
nevertheless the Lord's counsel—that will stand.
The fear of the Lord leads to life,
and he who has it will abide in satisfaction;
He will not be visited with evil.
—Proverbs 19:17–19, 20–21, 23 (NKJV)

Our hearts are always with the poor and their needs. The poor are always with us on the mission field or in our neighborhoods. We are rich beyond measure because Jesus is our Lord and King.

There is a period of time in our children's lives from infancy to adolescence when we have their ear. It is to be a time of encouragement, love, and correction. The teen years are often a separation and independence, so we have to act quickly. It is very important that we lead them to the Lord and provide sound Christian teaching.

There are many plans within our hearts, but the Lord's plan is the best. If we will listen to His voice, we will hear and abide to the best counsel. This is how we gain wisdom in our latter days. It is in that place of fellowship with the Lord that we find life, peace, and satisfaction. And He will lead us out of temptation and from all evil.

Step 175

Counsel in the heart of man is like deep water,
but a man of understanding will draw it out.
The righteous man walks in his integrity;
His children are blessed after him.
The hearing ear and the seeing eye,
the Lord has made them both.
There is gold and a multitude of rubies,
but the lips of knowledge are a precious jewel.
Plans are established by counsel;
By wise counsel wage war.
—Proverbs 20:5, 7, 12, 15, 18 (NKJV)

We are to be open to wise counsel and store it up deep within us. When the situation requires it, we draw it out and apply it to the problem. This way we avoid making foolish mistakes. Our battle is not against flesh and blood but the devil. Our strategy is formed from the wisdom of the Holy Spirit.

We are to walk in integrity at all times. Our children are watching our actions and listening to our voices. The child who follows a wise parent is blessed.

When we can see and hear in the Spirit, we are equipped for revelation of the future. We seek truth and avoid the pitfalls of only following our natural senses. God is wanting to take us into the deeper things beyond the simple. When we visit that special place, we have found a treasure chest of jewels. And now we can be an oracle of God blessing others.

Step 176

● ●

> A man's steps are of the Lord;
> How then can a man understand his own way?
> The spirit of a man is the lamp of the Lord,
> Searching all the inner depths of his heart.
> Mercy and truth preserve the king,
> and by lovingkindness he upholds his throne.
> The glory of young men is their strength,
> and the splendor of old men is their gray head.
> —Proverbs 20:24, 27–29 (NKJV)

Our steps are ordered by the Lord, and He guides us in the direction to go. He advises us when to stay and when to go. The wise man allows the Holy Spirit to show him the way, and he decides that this is the best way to live his life.

Those who don't know the Lord allow their spirit to be directed by selfish and soulish decisions. But we who are followers of Christ have a fire in our spirit that is in contact with the Holy Spirit. He knows and speaks to us in our hearts.

Enlightened husbands and wives rule their homes and families in mercy and truth. Business owners and bosses who are successful manage in the same way. National leaders who are wise oversee the people in mercy and truth. Godly truth and decisions set them apart.

The young man who is strong realizes he lacks wisdom that can only be gained through training and experience. He matures quickly when he acknowledges that God gives him life and strength. The old man knows that his physical and mental abilities are declining but can speak wisdom into a variety of situations.

Step 177

● ●

The king's heart is in the hand of the Lord, like the
rivers of water; He turns it wherever He wishes.
Every way of a man is right in his own eyes,
but the Lord weighs the hearts.
To do righteousness and justice
is more acceptable to the Lord than sacrifice.
The plans of the diligent lead surely to plenty,
but those of everyone who is hasty, surely to poverty.
—Proverbs 21:1–3, 5 (NKJV)

We are kings and priests in the hands of the Lord. Our lives are under the direction of the Lord, and He influences every important decision we make. We flow like a river, ever moving forward, headed toward a destination guided by the Holy Spirit.

If we ignore the counsel of the Lord, then we are on our own when we make choices. And when things don't go right, we cannot blame anyone but ourselves. Lord, give us a pure and sanctified heart unto You.

Obedience and attention to the Lord's wisdom is better than sacrifice. God is looking for those who will seek Him and do what He has called them to do. We are those who follow the Lord's leading and are committed to building His kingdom here on earth.

We will listen to the Lord and follow His instructions. Although we sometimes get in a hurry, we know that patience and waiting on the Lord is the best call. His timing is the best and takes into consideration factors we cannot imagine because He sees the big picture. So we rest and listen for His voice. As a result, we see ourselves growing in prosperity.

Step 178

• •

A gift in secret pacifies anger, and a bribe behind the back,
strong wrath. It is a joy for the just to do justice,
but destruction will come to the workers of iniquity.
There is desirable treasure,
and oil in the dwelling of the wise,
but a foolish man squanders it.
He who follows righteousness and mercy
finds life, righteousness and honor.
A wise man scales the city of the mighty,
and brings down the trusted stronghold.
—Proverbs 21:14–15, 20–22 (NKJV)

It seems like everyone enjoys being recognized with a surprise gift. It has the power to calm an angry mood. When we give it in secret, it lifts us up and brings a smile to our face.

We are the just who deal fairly with others, and it's powerful when it's done from a joyful heart. We operate from a heart that is wise and set apart for the Lord. God prospers us in our comings and goings.

It is by the mercy of God that we have been called righteous in His sight. Because we have right standing in the sight of God, we have been honored with true life, riches, and wisdom.

The devil hates our righteousness and will try to steal, kill, and destroy us. We have the power of God working on our side and are strengthened by the Holy Spirit. He establishes and equips us to go after and fulfill our destiny. Nothing will keep us from fulfilling the call and plan of God on our lives. If we need to scale a wall or overcome some barrier, we will accomplish it by putting our faith and trust in God.

Step 179

Whoever guards his mouth and tongue
keeps his soul from troubles.
A wicked man hardens his face,
but as for the upright, he establishes his way.
There is no wisdom or understanding
or counsel against the Lord.
The horse is prepared for the day of battle,
but deliverance is of the Lord.
—Proverbs 21:23, 29–31 (NKJV)

We know there is power in the tongue to bring life or death. When we guard our tongue, we are slow to speak and to listen carefully. Our mouths speak what's in our hearts, so we strive to speak positively and constructively.

We face the challenges of life as opportunities for upgrade in our way. Our focus is on honoring Jesus and walking in the light. His life is a model for ours and a template for loving others unconditionally.

Who dares speak against the Lord's counsel? He sees the whole picture and desires the best for us. When we find ourselves moving contrary to the Lord's leading, then it's time to pause and gather some new thoughts.

The horse and rider may be armored and prepared for battle, but it is the Lord who has defeated the enemy. Our armor is mostly defensive with only sword of the Spirit for offense. The war has been won by Jesus it's up to us to enforce the victory over the devil.

Step 180

• •

A good name is to be chosen rather than great riches, loving
favor rather than silver and gold. The rich and the poor have
this in common, the Lord is the maker of them all. A prudent
man foresees evil and hides himself, but the simple pass on and
are punished. By humility and the fear of the Lord are riches
and honor and life. Thorns and snares are in the way of the
perverse; He who guards his soul will be far from them.
—Proverbs 22:1–5 (NKJV)

Our name is a good name because it is our given name. We are
unique, and there is no one else like us. God created us in His image
and knew us before we were born. And it because of the love of Jesus
that we have been born again. It's almost like we should get new
names because we are not the same persons that we were before Jesus
saved us and gave us new lives.

Our financial standing does not give us a higher or lower place
in the family of God. He loves us all equally. We are all servants of the
Most High God and called to honor Him with our lives. God also
loves the atheist and the evolutionist even though they don't believe
He exists or created them.

The reformed alcoholic probably shouldn't visit a tavern. He
has learned to avoid all temptation so as not to return to his old habits. With addictions, it's important that we lean on the Holy Spirit to
keep us out of the way of thorns and snares.

It is by reverence for the Lord and humility that we live each day.
We recognize that this is the doorway to riches, honor, and true life.

Step 181

●●●●●●●●●●●●●●●●●●●●●●●●●●●●●●●●

> Train up a child in the way he should go,
> And when he is old he will not depart from it.
> The rich rules over the poor,
> And the borrower is servant to the lender.
> He who has a generous eye will be blessed,
> For he gives of his bread to the poor.
> He who loves purity of heart
> And has grace on his lips,
> The king will be his friend.
> —Proverbs 22:6–7, 9, 11 (NKJV)

We who were raised by Christian parents and were brought up in a Christian home are blessed. That training and love for the Lord is deep within our hearts and will be remembered and applied one day.

Whenever possible, we are to save and pay cash for our big purchases. It is a wandering eye that wants something out of our price range and will borrow to have it. Enduring all the payments later on is a burden that should be avoided.

The work of the soup kitchen and the clothes closet are to be blessed with our generosity whenever possible. The institution that can provide rent money to the poor is an asset to the community. Let's give to them out of our abundance because God will compensate us.

When we maintain a pure heart and speak words of love, kindness, and goodness to others, we are a blessing to the Lord. Those qualities will draw us to like-minded people and be a source of lasting friendships.

Step 182

The eyes of the Lord preserve knowledge,
But He overthrows the words of the faithless.
Incline your ear and hear the words of the wise,
And apply your heart to my knowledge;
For it is a pleasant thing if you keep them within you;
Let them all be fixed upon your lips,
So that your trust may be in the Lord;
I have instructed you today, even you.
—Proverbs 22:12, 17–19 (NKJV)

The eyes of the Lord are upon us. He constantly keeps watch over us. This knowledge is too wonderful to imagine. The Holy Spirit is ever guarding us from danger and comforting us in disappointment. He is available to show the deeper things of God for those who hunger and thirst after that kind of knowledge.

It is impossible to please God without faith. The faithless do not believe in Him, can't imagine a personal relationship, or a heavenly Father who loves them.

We incline our ears to hear the wise teachings of the Lord from His Word. Our hearts delight in the good news! If we listen carefully, He will speak to us in the stillness some amazing revelations.

It is out of pure hearts open to the revelations of heaven that we can speak words of knowledge into the atmosphere. Earthly knowledge is good but to seek the things of God is even better.

We will put our trust in the Lord today and every day. We know now that His Word can be trusted, and that it brings strength into our lives. We are people of faith and know that it connects us with the Almighty who knows all things. When we study His Word, we will look for application of truth for today. We put our faith in the wisdom of God.

Step 183

Have I not written to you excellent things.
Of counsels and knowledge,
That I may make you know the certainty of the words of truth,
That you may answer words of truth
To those who send to you?
Do not remove the ancient landmark
Which your fathers have set.
Do you see a man who excels in his work?
He will stand before kings;
He will not stand before unknown men.
—Proverbs 22:20–21, 28–29 (NKJV)

God has communicated to us excellent things through King Solomon and the Holy Spirit. We are blessed to have such good counsel and knowledge from the Word of God. It's easy to study scripture today with all the different Bible versions and commentaries.

The purpose of our study is to learn and apply God's truth. For those who question our beliefs, we are equipped to give an answer for the hope that lies within us. When that heavenly knowledge is within us, there is a boldness and confidence that surrounds us.

We are to build on what Christians learned and taught in the past. We do not despise their understanding but attempt to stand on their shoulders and reach higher. Each day is an opportunity to become a little wiser and grow to maturity in Christ.

We are to use the gifts and talents that God has given us. This is the way we can fulfill our unique place in the kingdom. Each Christian has an obligation to serve the Lord in whatever capacity he or she is called to fill.

Step 184

Apply your heart to instruction, And your
ears to words of knowledge.
My son, if your heart is wise,
My heart will rejoice—indeed, I myself;
Yes, my inmost being will rejoice
When your lips speak right things.
Do not let your heart envy sinners,
But be zealous for the fear of the Lord all the day;
For surely there is a hereafter,
And your hope will not be cut off.
Hear, my son, and be wise;
And guide your heart in the way.
—Proverbs 23:12, 15–19 (NKJV)

We are the saints who hear the words of instruction and knowledge but also apply it in our lives. We are known as people who have wise hearts because we are filled with the Word of God. All the witnesses in heaven rejoice each time the wisdom of God is spoken from our lips.

We don't have a wealth of material things nor do we desire them. We have a few things, but those things don't have us. Our neighbors may have the latest or the greatest, but we don't envy or criticize them.

Each day, we live in reverence, honor, and thankfulness of the Lord and what He has accomplished for us. The world and the lost cannot have a hope for the future until they accept Jesus as their Lord and Savior. It is clear from the Bible that there is a heaven and a hell. Because of Jesus whom we love and adore, we are assured of eternity in heaven and are forever grateful.

Step 185

• •

Buy the truth, and do not sell it, Also wisdom and instruction
and understanding. The father of the righteous will greatly rejoice,
And he who begets a wise child will delight in him. Let your father
and your mother be glad, And let her who bore you rejoice. My
son, give me your heart, And let your eyes observe my ways.
—Proverbs 23:23–26 (NKJV)

The truth of God is to be absorbed and retained in us like a valuable treasure. Wise instruction and understanding are to be stored up
inside of us and to be used and applied liberally to life's situations.
God's wisdom is not like a book to be read and forgotten but to be
made available to anyone who would ask.

Wise parents are to be honored and obeyed. They have wisdom and experience that are valuable. We have a heavenly Father
who greatly rejoices in us and delights in giving us the desires of our
hearts. The teachings and ways of the Lord Jesus Christ are to be
observed and followed from hearts that are given over to Him.

We are to live our lives in a way that makes our mother and
earthly father proud. Good parents invest and sacrifice for their children. We are to be parents who love and care for our children and our
children's children. The Holy Spirit is our teacher. He will make the
wisdom of God available to us.

Step 186

• •

Through wisdom a house is built, And by understanding
it is established; By knowledge the rooms are filled
With all precious and pleasant riches.
A wise man is strong,
Yes, a man of knowledge increases strength;
For by wise counsel you will wage your own war,
And in a multitude of counselors there is safety.
My son, eat honey because it is good,
And the honeycomb which is sweet to your taste;
So shall the knowledge of wisdom be to your soul;
If you have found it, there is a prospect,
And your hope will not be cut off.
—Proverbs 24:3–6, 13–14 (NKJV)

The wisdom of God strengthens our lives and fills our homes with precious and pleasant riches. Our knowledge and relationship with Jesus Christ are a sweet-smelling aroma to the Father. The Word of God is filled with a sweet taste that satisfies our souls. There is safety and hope in God's wisdom. Searching for knowledge and understanding is like digging for buried treasure and finding it.

When we wear the belt of truth and the rest of the armor, we are protected from every attack of the enemy. We know that Jesus defeated the devil at the cross. The Word of God has power over every accusation of the enemy. When we are filled with scripture, then we are equipped for every situation that life might bring our way.

Step 187

It is the glory of God to conceal a matter, But the glory of kings is to search out a matter. As the heavens for height and the earth for depth, So the heart of kings is unsearchable. Take away the dross from silver, And it will go to the silversmith for jewelry. Take away the wicked from before the king, And his throne will be established in righteousness. Do not exalt yourself in the presence of the king, And do not stand in the place of the great; For it is better that he say to you, "Come up here," Than that you should be put lower in the presence of the prince, Whom your eyes have seen.

—Proverbs 25:2–7 (NKJV)

God has hidden things from us that we cannot see on our own. However, God does not keep things from us but for us. We must search them out through intimacy and fellowship with Him. With the help of the Holy Spirit, the mysterious and deeper things of God become uncovered.

In our own righteousness, we are unworthy to stand before God. But through the washing of the water and the blood, we have been made clean. The throne room of heaven has been opened to us by Jesus Christ. Just as the curtain to the holy of holies was torn open, Christ has opened up heaven to His followers.

Self-righteousness will never gain us salvation. It is only by accepting the gift of righteousness from Christ that we are accepted in the beloved.

Step 188

A word fitly spoken is like apples of gold
In settings of silver.
Like an earring of gold and an ornament of fine gold
is a wise rebuker to an obedient ear.
Like the cold of snow in time of harvest
is a faithful messenger to those who send him,
For he refreshes the soul of his masters.
By long forbearance a ruler is persuaded,
And a gentle tongue breaks a bone.
—Proverbs 25:11–13, 15 (NKJV)

The Holy Spirit is faithful to give us the right words to speak at the right time. A word of encouragement can be a blessing to one who is without hope. A healing prayer can bring a miracle to the sick or diseased. A witness with the word of truth can affect the right outcome. A sermon message inspired by God can bring insight to the listening audience.

A prophetic word can open the ears and heart of the listener. Prophecy, healing, and discipleship did not end with the death of the close followers of Jesus. By the power, counsel, and wisdom of the Holy Spirit, we are equipped to help the weak, sick, and confused people of our day. It requires a pure and obedient spirit to hear from God and a boldness to speak it out.

We are wise when we don't rush in with a soothing word if emotions are heated. It is better to wait until tempers cool down. One who is willing to listen and be persuaded can receive our help. Our counsel may not be received the first time and persistence may be necessary. A soft and gentle voice can be most effective.

Step 189

● ●

> If your enemy is hungry, give him bread to eat;
> And if he is thirsty, give him water to drink;
> For so you will heap coals of fire on his head,
> And the Lord will reward you.
> It is better to dwell in a corner of a housetop,
> Than in a house shared with a contentious woman.
> As cold water to a weary soul,
> So is good news from a far country.
> It is not good to eat much honey;
> So to seek one's own glory is not glory.
> —Proverbs 25:21–22, 24–25, 27 (NKJV)

A kind word and a friendly greeting are appropriate for our enemy. A forgiving heart is the source for our words. We remember that we have wronged and hurt others, so forgiveness is our motto.

A spouse either man or woman who is contentious is difficult to live with. We are to do all in our power to reduce strife in the home. Of course, any physical and mental abuse is not to be tolerated. We just have to make sure we are not the cause of the strife and discontent.

Often, we hear good testimony from our brothers and sisters in Christ. We build upon that testimony so that we can give a good report. We remember that the Word of God is good news!

To seek our own glory is like pride before a fall. Jesus Christ is the only One who gets the glory. There is no comparison between our lives and the life of our Savior. We can only thank Him for what He has done for us and seek to honor Him always.

Step 190

Do not boast about tomorrow,
For you do not know what a day may bring forth.
Let another man praise you, and not your own mouth;
A stranger, and not your own lips.
Open rebuke is better
Than love carefully concealed.
Faithful are the wounds of a friend, But the
kisses of an enemy are deceitful.
—Proverbs 27:1–2, 5–6 (NKJV)

We do not worry or boast about tomorrow because we don't know what it might bring. Instead, we focus on today and live in the present. Tomorrow may bring relief and good tidings, but we don't count on it until today has passed, and tomorrow becomes today.

It is prideful to brag about ourselves. Let us focus on the needs and accomplishments of others, praising them instead of ourselves. If others see the good that we do, then let them be the first to speak of it.

It is better for us to receive criticism out of love and concern than to be ignored. We have an opportunity to grow and mature when others who see our faults point them out. We are sometimes blinded to the hurt and confusion we create.

Our enemies are likely to lie to us or sweet talk us. We must be on guard when their words do not line up with the truth or reality. Our friends are the ones who speak honestly, positively, and lovingly to us.

Step 191

• •

Ointment and perfume delight the heart, And the sweetness of a man's friend gives delight by hearty counsel. Do not forsake your own friend or your father's friend, Nor go to your brother's house in the day of your calamity; Better is a neighbor nearby than a brother far away. My son, be wise, and make my heart glad, That I may answer him who reproaches me. A prudent man foresees evil and hides himself; The simple pass on and are punished.
—Proverbs 27:9–12 (NKJV)

What a joy it is to have close friends. We enjoy spending time with them and share in their ups and downs. A good friend listens to us and shares personal hopes, dreams, and concerns. We know we can share deep things and are sure we can trust and confide in that friend.

We spend time with friends and family not just at funerals or weddings. Relationships require time and effort to be built up; they don't just happen. A little sacrifice on our part will go a long way toward a lasting relationship. An investment in our neighbors pays off. If we want to be loved, we must give love.

We are to honor and thank our parents whenever possible. Let's be good sons and daughters that make our parents proud.

We are those who are not lazy but prepare for a rainy day. It is prudent to care for and maintain our dwelling. We exercise and eat right to keep our bodies fit. We read and study to keep our minds sound. We are alert to temptations and on guard to stay out of sin. We put a little money aside in savings to prevent problems during an economic downturn.

Step 192

• •

As iron sharpens iron,
So a man sharpens the countenance of his friend.
Whoever keeps the fig tree will eat its fruit;
So he who waits on his master will be honored.
As in water face reflects face,
So a man's heart reveals the man.
The refining pot is for silver and the furnace for gold,
And a man is valued by what others say of him.
—Proverbs 27:17–19, 21 (NKJV)

Even though we make every effort to follow the leading of the Holy Spirit, we sometimes go astray. God uses friends and family to point out our wanderings and advise us in the way to go. So wise counsel is not to be ignored or despised.

We know if we care for a plant with good soil, water, sunlight, and tender loving care, it will flourish. The same is true with those who are over us. If we honor and respect them, our relationship is more likely to prosper.

When we look in the mirror, we see a reflection of ourselves. When God looks upon us, He sees our heart. The heart is the very core and essence of who we are. It is through God's loving-kindness and grace that He considers our countenance.

The circumstances of life and how we deal with them reveals who we are and who we are becoming. It is often like a refiner's fire that is burning away the dross. God didn't promise us a rose garden, but we can plant roses wherever we are.

Step 193

●●●●●●●●●●●●●●●●●●●●●●●●●●●●●●

Be diligent to know the state of your flocks, And attend to your
herds; For riches are not forever, Nor does a crown endure to all
generations. When the hay is removed, and the tender grass shows
itself, And the herbs of the mountains are gathered in, The lambs
will provide your clothing, And the goats the price of a field;
You shall have enough goats' milk for your food, For the food of
your household, And the nourishment of your maidservants.
—Proverbs 27:23–27 (NKJV)

A pastor knows and cares for his congregation. Jesus heals our sicknesses and diseases. By His stripes, we are healed and made whole.
The Holy Spirit tends to our wounds and afflictions. Under the
wings of the Almighty, we are protected and safe.

We have an obligation to God to save and spend carefully what
He has provided for us. He has prospered us so that we might give
into the kingdom and further the work of ministry. We do not have
the right to spend foolishly or frivolously what God has given us.

We are blessed to have our needs met and most of our wants.
Let us be generous to give to other ministries what is leftover. Jesus
fed the five thousand with some fish and bread, and there was plenty.
We may not have a lot, but what we do have might be a blessing to
someone else.

Step 194

The wicked flee when no one pursues,
But the righteous are bold as a lion.
Because of the transgression of a land, many are its princes;
But by a man of understanding and knowledge
Right will be prolonged.
Those who forsake the law praise the wicked,
But such as keep the law contend with them.
Evil men do not understand justice,
But those who seek the Lord understand all.
Better is the poor who walks in his integrity
Than one perverse in his ways, though he be rich.
—Proverbs 28:1–2, 4–6 (NKJV)

We are the righteous who do not fear and are bold as lions. Just ask us, and we will tell you that we love and follow Jesus. We have found a new life in our Savior that is no comparison to the old one. And if you are open and ready, we will tell you how you can become a disciple of Jesus Christ.

We are those who proclaim righteousness and justice by following the teachings of Jesus Christ. The Word of God is good news and the standard by which all men can prosper. We follow the law of the land and report to a higher authority, the One who created the heavens and the earth.

We seek to understand God's system of justice and to know His truth. It is a system and a standard of honesty and integrity. When we walk in His integrity, we are rich beyond measure. The Christian life is full of love, joy, and peace that is hopeful beyond an unbeliever's understanding.

Step 195

Whoever keeps the law is a discerning son,
But a companion of gluttons shames his father.
One who increases his possessions by usury and extortion
Gathers it for him who will pity the poor.
Whoever causes the upright to go astray in an evil way,
He himself will fall into his own pit;
But the blameless will inherit good.
The rich man is wise in his own eyes,
But the poor who has understanding searches him out.
When the righteous rejoice, there is great glory;
But when the wicked arise, men hide themselves.
—Proverbs 28:7–8, 10–12 (NKJV)

We are those who love the Word of God and keep it in our hearts. We love the sinner but hate the sin. The world makes fun of the Lord and laughs at the gospel. We will not be moved when someone criticizes the church, but we will stand firmly for the work of ministry.

The wealth of the wicked is stored up for the righteous. We are those who stand united in the work of the kingdom. We will help the poor in any way we can. Our inheritance is prosperity here on earth and riches in heaven.

The righteous, rich or poor, stand strong in the lean or boom times. To be wealthy without God in our lives is a formula for destruction and failure. There is a place in our hearts that only the love and presence of Jesus Christ can fill. The shed blood of Jesus is the only thing that can cover us from the attacks of the enemy. That blood has washed us clean from any sin debt we owed.

Step 196

He who covers his sins will not prosper,
But whoever confesses and forsakes them will have mercy.
Happy is the man who is always reverent,
But he who hardens his heart will fall into calamity.
A ruler who lacks understanding is a great oppressor,
But he who hates covetousness will prolong his days.
Whoever walks blamelessly will be saved,
But he who is perverse in his ways will suddenly fall.
—Proverbs 28:13–14, 16, 18 (NKJV)

There is no work we can do to gain our salvation but only to believe. We know the blood of Jesus has covered our sins and washed us clean. So we regularly confess our sins and receive atonement from the sacrifice of Jesus Christ. It is by the mercy and grace of God we are able to walk in freedom and victory.

What a joy it is to walk in close relationship and partnership with the Holy Spirit. There is no better companion to comfort and guide us through the circumstances of life. He is the best friend we could ever have. So throughout the day, we praise and thank him.

Those who delight themselves in the Lord will have the desires of their hearts fulfilled. We line up our desires with the desires of heaven. What someone else has that we lack does not interest us. We are more than blessed by God.

We will walk all the days of our lives in honesty and integrity. Our salvation has been purchased by our Lord Jesus, and we do all we can to protect and preserve it. It is a valuable gift and hope for the future. Salvation is not something we could have gained on our own, and so we are forever indebted to our Lord.

Step 197

He who tills his land will have plenty of bread,
But he who follows frivolity will have poverty enough!
A faithful man will abound with blessings,
But he who hastens to be rich will not go unpunished.
He who is of a proud heart stirs up strife,
But he who trusts in the Lord will be prospered.
He who trusts in his own heart is a fool,
But whoever walks wisely will be delivered.
When the wicked arise, men hide themselves;
But when they perish, the righteous increase.
—Proverbs 28:19–20, 25–26, 28 (NKJV)

We are to be thankful for the job/work we have that pays the bills as long as we are able. If we should happen to become wealthy, then it is an opportunity to give into ministry and to the poor.

Our trust and hope are in the Lord. He is the source for our prosperity. It is not about who we are but who Christ is in us. We choose to be humble rather than proud. We avoid being the source of strife in our relationships.

As we walk in the Spirit, we know we are delivered and protected from every attack of the enemy. He hates our confidence and boldness in the Lord. It is for wisdom we live, move, and have our being in the Lord.

The wicked do not understand or desire a fellowship with our Lord and Savior. The have aligned themselves with Satan out of ignorance and foolishness. Their focus is on themselves and riches through pride and frivolity. Our desire is for them to be saved and to come into the kingdom. We will do what we can to help and show them a better way.

Step 198

• •

When the righteous are in authority, the people rejoice;
But when a wicked man rules, the people groan.
Whoever loves wisdom makes his father rejoice,
But a companion of harlots wastes his wealth.
The king establishes the land by justice,
But he who receives bribes overthrows it.
By transgression an evil man is snared,
But the righteous sings and rejoices.
The righteous considers the cause of the poor,
But the wicked does not understand such knowledge.
—Proverbs 29:2–4, 6–7 (NKJV)

When there are Christians in authority, there is rejoicing. However, not all are happy about it and will seek to criticize and undermine the leaders. The righteous leaders are entrusted to rule with wisdom and fairness. The good ones seek God's direction and the counsel of advisors who hear from God. They spend time in prayer and study of the Word. Their decisions reflect the wisdom of God and His righteousness. These leaders are not immune to the attacks of the devil but resist him so that they are not corrupted.

To walk with the Holy Spirit unlocks the supernatural joy of the Lord. It causes us to break out in songs of praise and words of thankfulness. There is freedom knowing we are saved and washed clean in the blood of Christ.

We are aware of the plight of the poor and know that it is by the grace of God we are not poor too. There is a mentality of poverty that must be broken and overcome through the power and wisdom of the Word of God. It could be a curse that must be broken or a change of thinking. When we see ourselves as children of God and righteous before Him, then we have begun our journey out of poverty.

Step 199

Scoffers set a city aflame,
But wise men turn away wrath.
The bloodthirsty hate the blameless,
But the upright seek his well-being.
A fool vents all his feelings,
But a wise man holds them back.
The poor man and the oppressor have this in common:
The Lord gives light to the eyes of both.
The king who judges the poor with truth,
His throne will be established forever.
—Proverbs 29:8, 10–11, 13–14 (NKJV)

Divisive issues separate good people and stir up hate and discontent. A nation's worst enemy is not from the outside but within her borders. Godly principles accepted by a majority can quell an uprising. One of the enemy's greatest weapons is division within marriages, families, cities, and nations.

The unconditional love of God brings peace and joy. Our soulish emotions and thoughts can separate us from God. Not every emotion has to be expressed especially when it stirs up hate. We are to let the Holy Spirit look in our hearts and determine if there are any wrong thoughts there. The foolish decisions we make are without the influence of the Holy Spirit. We are commanded to love our enemies. We are to love the sinner but hate the sin.

The Lord makes His wisdom available to the rich and the poor. It is when we walk in His light that we see issues and problems clearly. We are directed by the Holy Spirit to the ways of truth, and there we find peace, hope, and joy.

Step 200

● ●

Where there is no revelation, the people cast off restraint;
But happy is he who keeps the law.
A man's pride will bring him low,
But the humble in spirit will retain honor.
The fear of man brings a snare,
But whoever trusts in the Lord shall be safe.
Many seek the ruler's favor,
But justice for man comes from the Lord.
An unjust man is an abomination to the righteous,
And he who is upright in the way is an abomination to the wicked.
—Proverbs 29:18, 23, 25–27 (NKJV)

God speaks to us through His Word and in a still small voice. For those who listen, there is fresh revelation from the Lord. God has not stopped speaking to His people since Christ ascended into heaven. Naysayers will not hear His voice and will deprive themselves of this blessing.

To be humble in spirit is a great asset in this life. Pride comes before a fall and relies on self-righteousness to sustain it. There is a better way which provides safety and favor when we depend wholly on the Lord.

We who are upright tend to offend the unrighteous. We don't depend on the ways of the world and instead display love, joy, peace, and hope. God's ways are higher than our ways. We seek a fellowship and intimacy with the Lord that baffles the lost. We don't go out of our way to offend them, but sometimes just being a Christian angers them. Just because we are unaccepted by some unbelievers is no reason to give up the glorious relationship we have with Jesus.

Step 201

• •

Who has ascended into heaven, or descended? Who has gathered
the wind in His fists? Who has bound the waters in a garment?
Who has established all the ends of the earth? What is His name,
and what is His Son's name, If you know? Every word of God
is pure; He is a shield to those who put their trust in Him.
—Proverbs 30:4–5 (NKJV)

Jesus Christ has descended and taken the keys of captivity. He is also
the One who has ascended into heaven and sits at the right hand of
the Father. He is the One who hears our prayers of help and suppli-
cation. He has ascended but also resides in the heart of every believer.

Jesus Christ is the all-powerful God of the universe. All of
heaven and earth were made by Him and for Him. It is through Him
that the sun rises every morning, and all life gets it nourishment. He
is the author of life past, present, and future. All who put their trust
in Him will one day see Him face-to-face and spend eternity with
Him.

He is the Creator of the lands and the oceans. We stand in awe
of the immensity of the waters and the expanse of the land. There is
life and beauty in all He has made. We see His handwriting in the
colors of the sunrise and sunset.

All scripture is inspired by God and is pure and living. He has
given us everything we need in His Word for life, health, and prosperity. We are not to add to it or delete any of it but to feed on it to
overflowing. In Him, we put our complete faith and trust.

Step 202

Who can find a virtuous wife?
For her worth is far above rubies.
The heart of her husband safely trusts her;
So he will have no lack of gain.
She does him good and not evil
All the days of her life.
She extends her hand to the poor,
Yes, she reaches out her hands to the needy.
—Proverbs 31:10–12, 20 (NKJV)

A wise man knows that to find a virtuous woman is a treasure indeed. He appreciates her love for him and returns even more love to her. He depends on her and trusts her counsel in difficult situations. Their marriage is a partnership where each builds the other up. A husband and his wife who trust each other will be successful in all their endeavors. Together they will serve the Lord and raise their children to do so likewise.

A virtuous wife honors her husband and cares for him and her family with all her ability. She uses her gifts and talents to serve her family and others. She is loved and appreciated by all who come to know her.

She goes out of her way to help the poor and needy. She evaluates her resources and gives to the needy. She creates a home that is a prosperous and abundant resource for others. She is known for her creativity and love to others in need. A good wife brings joy, happiness, and encouragement into the home. She does it all out of a love for God, her family, and people in her life.

Step 203

● ●

Strength and honor are her clothing;
She shall rejoice in time to come.
She opens her mouth with wisdom,
And on her tongue is the law of kindness.
Her children rise up and call her blessed;
Her husband also, and he praises her:
Charm is deceitful and beauty is passing,
But a woman who fears the Lord, she shall be praised.
—Proverbs 31:25-26, 28, 30 (NKJV)

The woman of God finds her strength in the Lord. She honors and praises Her Lord and Master, who honors and praises her. She praises Him now and forever. She finds joy and strength in her walk with the Holy Spirit.

Wisdom and kindness are two powerful attributes of the woman of God. She has learned them through a loving relationship with Jesus. When she speaks, it is to bring wise counsel and encouragement to those around her.

She creates a peaceful home for her family. They appreciate her work and creativity. Her children are the fruit of her labors. Her husband loves and adores her as a special gift from God.

The charm of a woman can be alluring, and her beauty fill the eye. But the true beauty is in her heart which is given over to the Lord. Out of her heart spring honest thoughts, and out of her mouth are words of wisdom. Because she is connected to the Lord, her countenance is a blessing to all.

About the Author

The author of *Stepping through the Psalms and the Proverbs* is Alan Robert Engle, a retired pastor of Laramie Christian Center, Laramie, Wyoming. He has two daughters and a son who are grown and out on their own. Alan has a master's degree in divinity from Christian Bible College in Rocky Mount, North Carolina, and a Master of Arts degree in Education from University of Colorado. Alan is a life coach training through Bethel Coaching. Spending time with the Holy Spirit brings him great joy and peace. He enjoys special moments with his grandson, Axel. His main hobby is exploring mountain trails in God's creation. It is in those hours that he is refreshed and recharged enjoying intimacy with God. He is involved in prayer and healing ministry at Bethel church. Alan resides in Redding, California, and attends Bethel church.

CPSIA information can be obtained
at www.ICGtesting.com
Printed in the USA
LVHW091917160321
681581LV00077B/414